LARRY DEXTER'S GREAT SEARCH

OR

THE HUNT FOR THE MISSING MILLIONAIRE

HOWARD R. GARIS

[ZHINGOORA BOOKS]

PREFACE

Dear Boys:

I hope you will be glad to read of the further adventures of Larry Dexter. He has made some progress since you first made his acquaintance in the book "From Office Boy to Reporter." He has also advanced in his chosen profession from the days when he did his first news-gathering for the *Leader*. In this volume he is sent on a "special assignment," as it is called. He has to find a New York millionaire who has mysteriously disappeared.

How Larry solved the strange secret, I have woven into a story that I trust will be liked by all the boys who read it. I have taken many incidents from real life for this story, using some of my own experiences while a newspaper reporter as a basis for facts.

The things that happened to Larry are not at all out of the ordinary among reporters. The life has many strange surprises in it. If I have been able to set them down in a way that will please you boys, and if you enjoy following the further fortunes of Larry Dexter, I shall feel amply repaid for my efforts on this volume.

Yours sincerely,

HOWARD R. GARIS.

CONTENTS

CHAPTER I

THE WRECK

Into the city room of the New York *Leader* hurried Mr. Whiggen, the telegraph editor. In his hand was a slip of paper, containing a few typewritten words. Mr. Whiggen laid it on the desk of Bruce Emberg, the city editor.

"Just came in over our special wire," said Mr. Whiggen. "Looks as if it might be a bad wreck. That's a dangerous coast. I thought you might like to send one of your men down to cover it."

"Thanks," replied the city editor. "I will. Let's see," and, while he read the message, a score of reporters in the room looked up to see what had caused the telegraph editor to come in with such a rush.

This is what Mr. Emberg read from the slip Mr. Whiggen handed him:

"BULLETIN.—S.S. *Olivia* ashore off Seven Mile Beach, on sand bar. Big steerage list, some cabin passengers—fruit cargo. Ship badly listed, but may get off at high tide. If not, liable to break up in storm. Passengers safe yet.—ASSOCIATED PRESS."

There followed a brief description of the vessel, compiled from the maritime register, giving her tonnage, size, and when built.

"Um," remarked Mr. Emberg when he had read the short message, which was what newspaper men call a "flash" or bulletin, intended to notify the journals of the barest facts of the story. "This looks as if it would amount to something. I'll send a man down. Have we any one there?"

"We've got a man in Ocean City," replied the telegraph editor, "but I'm afraid I can't reach him. Have to depend on the Associated Press until we can get some one down."

"All right, I'll send right away."

The telegraph editor went back to his sanctum on the run, for it was near first-edition time and he wanted to get a display head written for the wreck story. Mr. Emberg looked over the room, in which many reporters were at work, most of them typewriting stories as fast as their fingers could fly over the keys. Several of the news-gatherers who had heard the conversation between the two editors hoped they might be sent on that assignment, for though it meant hard work it was a chance to get out of the city for a while.

"Are you up, Newton?" asked Mr. Emberg of a reporter in the far corner of the room.

"No, I've got that political story to write yet."

"That's so. I can't spare you. How about you, Larry?"

"I'm up," was the answer, which is the newspaper man's way of saying his particular task is finished.

"Here, then, jump out on this," and the city editor handed the telegram to a tall, good-looking youth, who arose from his desk near a window.

Larry Dexter, who had risen from the rank of office boy to reporter, took in the message at a glance.

"Shall I start now?" he asked.

"As soon as you can get a train. Seven Mile Beach is down on the Jersey coast, near Anglesea. You can't get there in time to wire us anything for to-day, but rush a good story for to-morrow. If a storm comes up, and they have to rescue the passengers, it will make a corker. Don't be afraid of slinging your words if it turns out worth while. Here's an order on the cashier for some money. Hustle now," and Mr. Emberg scribbled down something on a slip of paper which he handed to the young reporter.

"Leave the message in the telegraph room as you go out," went on the city editor. "Mr. Whiggen may want it. Hustle now, Larry, and do your best."

Many envious eyes followed Larry Dexter as he hurried out of the city room, putting on his coat and hat as he went, for he had been working in his shirt sleeves.

Larry went down the long corridor, stopping in the telegraph room to leave the message which was destined to be responsible for his part in a series of strange events. He had little idea, as he left the *Leader* office that morning, that his assignment to get the story of the wreck was the beginning of a singular mystery.

Larry cashed the order Mr. Emberg had given him, and hurried to the railroad station. He found there was no train for an hour, and, telephoning to the city editor to that effect, received permission to go home and get some extra clothing, as he might have to stay away several days.

The young reporter rather startled his mother as he hurried in to tell her he was going out of town, but Mrs. Dexter had, in a measure, become used to her son doing all sorts of queer things since he had started in newspaper life.

"Will you be gone long, Larry?" she asked, as he kissed her good-bye, having packed a small valise.

"Can't say, mother. Probably not more than two days."

"Bring me some sea shells," begged Larry's brother, Jimmie, a bright little chap.

"And I want a lobster and a crab and a starfish," spoke Mary, a sunny-haired toddler.

"All right, and I'll bring Lucy some shells to make beads of," answered Larry, mentioning his older sister, who was not at home.

Larry found he had not much time left to catch his train, and he was obliged to hurry to the ferry which took him to Jersey City. There he boarded a Pennsylvania Railroad train, and was soon being whirled toward the coast.

Seven Mile Beach was a rather dangerous stretch of the Jersey shore, not far from Cape May. There were several lighthouses along it, but they did not always prevent vessels from running on a long sand bar, some distance out. More than one gallant ship had struck far up on it, and, being unable to get off, had been pounded to pieces by the waves.

By inquiring Larry found that the wreck of the *Olivia* was just off a lonely part of the coast, and that there were no railroad stations near it.

"Where had I better get off?" he asked, of the conductor.

"Well, you can get off at Sea Isle City, or Sackett's Harbor. Both stations are about five miles from where the ship lies, according to all accounts. Then you can walk."

"He can do better than that," interposed a brakeman.

"How?" asked Larry.

"There's a station, or rather what remains of it, half way between those places," the brakeman said. "It used to be called Miller's Beach. Started to be a summer resort, but it failed. There's nothing there now but a few fishermen's huts. But I guess that's nearer the wreck than Sea Isle City or Sackett's Harbor."

"Is there a place I could stay all night?" asked the young reporter.

"You might find a place. It's pretty lonesome. Sometimes, in the summer, there are campers there, but it's too late in the fall now to expect any of 'em. We'll stop there for water, and you can get off if you like."

Larry hardly knew what to do. Still he decided he was sent to get a story of the wreck, and he felt it would be well to get as near to it as possible. But there was another thing to think of, and that was how to get his news back into the *Leader* office. He must be near a telegraph station. Inquiry of the trainmen disclosed the fact that the nearest one was three miles from Miller's Beach.

"Guess I'll chance it," concluded Larry.

"We'll be there in an hour," went on the brakeman. "It's the jumping-off place, so to speak, and it's not going to be very pleasant there when the storm breaks."

That a heavy storm was gathering was all too evident from the mass of dark, rolling clouds in the east. They hung low, and there was a rising wind.

"I wouldn't want to be on that vessel," remarked the brakeman as the train, having stopped at a small station, started off again. "It's beginning to rain now, and it will blow great guns before morning."

Several men, their faces bronzed from exposure to the weather, had boarded the train. They talked quietly in one corner of the car.

"Who are they?" asked Larry, of the brakeman.

"Life savers, from the Anglesea station. Going to Tatums, I guess."

"What for?"

"Tatums is the life-saving station nearest where the vessel is ashore. Maybe they are going to help in case she breaks up in the storm. Tatums is about three miles below where you are going."

Larry began to see that he would have no easy task in getting news of the wreck, or in transmitting it after he had it. But he was not going to worry so early in the undertaking. So, when the brakeman warned him that the train was nearing the water tank, which was all that remained of interest to the railroad people at Miller's Beach, the young reporter prepared to alight.

As he went out on the platform the wind increased in violence, and then, with a rush and a roar, the rain began to fall in torrents.

Larry wished he could stay in the train, as he had no umbrella, but there was no help for it. He leaped off the platform of the car almost before it had stopped, and looked for a place of shelter. He was surprised to see several large buildings in front of him, but even through the mist of rain he noted that they were dilapidated and forsaken. He was in the midst of a deserted seaside resort.

He hurried on, being wet through before he had gone a dozen steps. Then he heard the train puffing away. It seemed as though he was left all alone in a very lonesome place.

"Hi! Where you going?" a voice hailed him.

Larry looked up, to see a man clad in yellow oilskins and rubber boots standing in front of him.

"I came down about the wreck," was the young reporter's reply.

"Got any folks aboard? If you have I'm sorry. She's broken her back!"

"No; I'm a reporter from New York. What do you mean about breaking her back?"

"Why, she ran away up on the bar at high tide. When it got low tide a while ago the bows and stern just sagged down, and she broke in two. They've got to work hard to save the passengers."

"That's a good story," was Larry's ejaculation, but it was not as heartless as it sounds, for he was only speaking professionally. "I must get down after it."

"What? With night coming on, the wreck almost half a mile out, and it coming on to blow like all possessed?" asked the man in oilskins. "Guess you don't know much about the sea, young man."

"Very little," answered Larry.

A sudden gust of wind, which dashed the rain with great force into his face, nearly carried the reporter off his feet. He looked about for a place of shelter.

"Better come with me," suggested the man. "There are no hotel accommodations here, though there once were. I have a shack down on the beach, and you're welcome to what I've got. I fish for a living. Bailey's my name. Bert Bailey."

"Go ahead. I'll follow," returned Larry. "I'd like to get out of this rain."

"Have to tog you out like me," said the old fisherman, as he led the youth toward his hut. "These are the only things for this weather."

As they hastened on there came over the water the boom of a signal gun from the wrecked steamer.

<hr>

CHAPTER II

ASHORE ON A RAFT

"What's that?" asked the young reporter, pausing.

"She's firing for help," replied the fisherman. "Can't last much longer now."

"Can't the life savers do anything?"

"They'll try, as soon as they can. Hard to get a boat off in this surf. It comes up mighty fast and heavy. Have to use the breeches buoy, I reckon. But come on, and I'll lend you some dry things to put on."

Five minutes later Larry was inside the hut. It was small, consisting of only two rooms, but it was kept as neatly as though it was part of a ship.

In a small stove there was a blazing fire of driftwood, and Larry drew near to the grateful heat, for, though it was only late in September, it was much colder at the beach than in the city, and he was chilly from the drenching.

"Lucky I happened to see you," Bailey went on. "I went down to the train to get my paper. One of the brakemen throws me one off each trip. It's all the news I get. I didn't expect any one down. This used to be quite a place years ago, but it's petered out. But come on, get your wet things off, and I'll see what I can do for you."

Larry was glad enough to do so. Fortunately he had brought some extra underwear in his valise, and, after a good rub-down before the stove, he donned the garments, and then put on a pair of the fisherman's trousers and an old coat, until his own clothes could dry.

As he sat before the stove, warm and comfortable after the drenching, and safe from the storm, which was now raging with increased fury outside, Larry heard the deep booming of the signal guns coming to him from across the angry sea.

"Are they in any danger?" he asked of Bailey, as the fisherman prepared to get a meal.

"Danger? There's always danger on the sea, my boy. I wouldn't want to be on that vessel, and I've been in some pretty tight places and gotten out again. She went ashore in a fog early this morning, but it will be a good while before she gets off. Seven Mile Beach hates to let go of a thing once it gets a hold."

It was getting dusk, and what little light of the fading day was left was obscured by the masses of storm clouds. The fisherman's hut was on the beach, not far from the high-water mark, and the booming of the surf on the shore came as a sort of melancholy accompaniment to the firing of the signal gun.

"Where is the wreck?" asked Larry, going to a window that looked out on the sea.

"Notice that black speck, right in line with my boat on the beach?" asked Bailey, pointing with a stubby forefinger over the young reporter's shoulder.

"That thing that looks like a seagull?"

"That's her. You can't see it very well on account of the rain, but there she lies, going to pieces fast, I'm afraid."

"Why didn't they get the people off before this?"

"Captain wouldn't accept help. Thought the vessel would float off and he'd save his reputation. The life savers went out when it was fairly calm, but didn't take anyone ashore. Now it's too late, I reckon."

As the fisherman spoke a rocket cleaved the fast-gathering blackness and shot up into the air.

"What's that?" asked Larry.

"She's firing signal lights. Wait and you'll see the coast-guard send up one in reply."

Presently a blue glare, up the beach not far from the cottage, shone amid the storm and darkness.

"That's George Tucker, burning a Coston light," explained Bailey. "He patrols this part of the beach to-night. They may try the boat again, but it's a risk."

There was an exchange of colored lights between the beach patrol and those on the steamer. Larry watched them curiously. He tried to picture the distress of those aboard the ship, waiting for help from shore; help that was to save them from the hungry waves all about.

"I wonder how I'm going to get news of this to the paper," Larry asked himself. He was beginning to feel quite worried, for he realized a great tragedy might happen at any moment, and he knew the *Leader* must have an account of it early the next morning, for it was an afternoon paper. The managing editor would probably order an extra.

"Couldn't I go down to the life-saving station?" asked Larry. "Maybe I could go out in a boat and get some news."

"They wouldn't let you, and, if they would, you couldn't send any news up to your paper from here to-night," replied the fisherman. "The nearest telegraph office is closed. Better stay here until morning. Then you can do something. I'll fix you up with oilskins after supper, if you like, and we'll go out on the beach. But I don't believe they'll launch the life-boat to-night."

The storm had now settled down into a fierce, steady wind and dashing rain. It fairly shook the little hut, and the stove roared with the draught created. Bailey soon had a hot meal ready, and Larry did full justice to it.

"Now we'll go out on the beach," the fisherman said, as he donned his oilskins, and got out a suit for Larry. The youth looked like anything but a reporter when he put on the boots and tied the yellow hat under his chin, for otherwise the wind would have whipped it off in an instant.

They closed up the hut, leaving a lantern burning in it, and started down toward the ocean. Through the darkness Larry could see a line of foam where the breakers struck the beach. They ran hissing over the pebbles and broken shells, and then surged back again. As the two walked along, a figure, carrying a lantern and clad as they were, in yellow oilskins, loomed up in the darkness.

"Hello, George!" cried Bailey, above the roar of the wind. "Going to get the boat out?"

"Not to-night. I signalled down to the station, but they flashed back that the surf was too high. We'll try the buoy in the morning, if the ship lasts that long, which I'm afraid she won't, for she's being pounded hard."

"The station where they keep the life-boat is about two miles below where we are now," Bailey explained to Larry. "We'll go down in the morning."

Suddenly a series of lights shot into the air from out at sea.

"What's that?" cried Larry.

"It's a signal that she's going to pieces fast!" cried the coast-guard. "Maybe we'll have to try the breeches buoy to-night. I must go to the station. They may need my help."

As the beach patrol hurried up the sandy stretch, Larry had half a notion to follow him. He wanted to see the operation of setting up the breeches buoy in order to make a good story, with plenty of details. He was about to propose to the fisherman that they go, when Bailey, who had gone down to the water's edge, uttered a cry.

"What is it?" called the reporter, hastening to the side of the old man.

"Looks like a life-raft from the steamer!" exclaimed Bailey. "She must have broken up. Maybe there's some one on this. Give me a hand. We'll try to haul it ashore when the next high wave sends it up on the beach."

Larry strained his eyes for a sight of the object. He could just discern something white, rising and falling on the tumultuous billows.

"Come on!" cried Bailey, rushing down into the first line of surf, as a big roller lifted the object and flung it onward. "Grab it and pull!"

Larry sprang down the sand. He waded out into the water, surprised to find how strong it was even in the shallow place. He made a grab for the dim white object. His hands grasped a rope. At the same time the fisherman got hold of another rope.

"Pull!" cried Bailey, and Larry bent his back in an effort to snatch the raft from the grip of the sea.

At first the waves shoved the raft toward them, then, as the waters receded, the current sucked it out again. But the fisherman was strong and Larry was no weakling. They hauled until they had the raft out of reach of the rollers. Then, while there came a wilder burst of the storm, and a dash of spray from the waves, Bailey leaned over the raft.

"There's a man lashed to it!" the fisherman cried. "We must get him to my shack and try to save him! Hurry now!"

CHAPTER III

THE MAN AT THE HUT

With a few quick strokes of his knife Bailey severed the ropes that bound the unconscious man to the raft. Then, taking him by the shoulders, and directing Larry to grasp the stranger's legs, they started for the hut.

"Queer there weren't more to come ashore on that raft," the fisherman remarked as they trudged over the sand. "It would hold a dozen with safety. Maybe they were all swept off but this one. Poor souls! there'll be many a one in Davy Jones's locker to-night I'm afraid."

"Is he—is he dead?" asked Larry, hesitatingly, for he had never handled a lifeless person before.

"I'm afraid so, but you never can tell. I've seen 'em stay under water a good while and brought back to life. You'd best help me carry him in, and then run for some of the life guards. I'll be working over him, and maybe I can bring him around."

Through the storm the two staggered with their burden. They reached the hut, and the man was tenderly placed on the floor near the fire.

"You hurry down the coast, and if you can see any of the guards tell 'em to come here," Bailey said to Larry. "They can't do anything for the wreck to-night."

Larry glanced at the man he had helped save from the sea. The stranger was of large size, and seemed well-dressed, though his clothes were anything but presentable now. His face was partly concealed by the collar of his coat, which was turned up, and Larry noted that the man had a heavy beard and moustache.

These details he took in quickly while he was buttoning his oilskin jacket tighter around his neck for another dash into the storm. Then, as he opened the door of the hut to go in search of a coast-guard, Bailey began to strip the wet garments from the unconscious man.

Larry was met by a heavy gust of wind and a dash of rain as he went outside again. He bent his head to the blast and made his way down the beach, the lantern he carried making fantastic shadows on the white sand.

He had not gone far before he saw a figure coming toward him. He waited, and in a few minutes was joined by George Tucker.

"Mr. Bailey wants you to come to his place and help him save a man who just came in on a raft," said Larry.

"Can't do it, my boy. I was just coming for him to help us launch the life-boat. We need all the men we can get, though we've got help from the station below us. Captain Needam sent me after Bailey."

"I don't believe he'll come," said Larry. "He'll not want to leave the man he pulled from the ocean."

"No, I don't s'pose he will," said George. "He may save a life. But we've got to try for the steamer. She's going to pieces, and there are many aboard of her, though I'm afraid there'll be fewer by morning."

"I'll come and help you," said the reporter. "I don't know much about life-boats, but I'm strong."

"Come along, then," said the coast guard.

They made their way down the beach, Larry accepting, in the manner newspaper reporters soon become accustomed to, the new rôle he was suddenly called on to play.

While he is thus journeying through the storm to aid in saving life, there will be an opportunity to tell you something about his past, and how he came to be a reporter on a leading New York newspaper.

Larry's introduction to a newspaper life was told of in the first volume of this series, entitled "From Office Boy to Reporter." At the start the youth lived with his mother, who was a widow, and his two sisters and a brother, on a farm in New York State.

The farm was sold for an unpaid mortgage after the death of Larry's father, and the little family came to New York to visit a sister of Mrs. Dexter, as Larry thought he could find work in the big city.

On their arrival they found that Mrs. Dexter's sister had unexpectedly gone out West to visit relatives, because of the sudden death of her husband. The Dexter family was befriended by a Mr. Jackson and his wife, and made the best of the situation. After many unsuccessful trials elsewhere, Larry got a position as office boy on the New York *Leader*.

His devotion to duty had attracted the attention of Harvey Newton, one of the "star" reporters on the sheet, and Mr. Emberg, the city editor, took a liking to Larry. In spite of the enmity of Peter Manton, another office boy on the same paper, Larry prospered. He was sent with Mr. Newton to report a big flood, and were there when a large dam broke, endangering many lives. Larry, who was sent to the telegraph office with an account of the accident, written by Mr. Newton on the spot, had an exciting race with Peter, who was then working for a rival newspaper. Larry won, and for his good work was advanced to be a regular reporter.

In the second volume of the series, entitled "Larry Dexter, Reporter," I told of his experiences as a gatherer of news in a great city.

In that book was related how Larry, with the aid of Mr. Newton, waged war against a gang of swindlers who were trying to rob the city, and, incidentally, Larry himself, for, as it developed, his mother had a deed to certain valuable property in the Bronx Park section of New York, and the swindlers desired to get possession of the land. They wanted to hold it and sell it to the city at a high price, but Larry got ahead of them.

To further their ends the bad men took away Jimmie, Larry's little brother, but the young reporter, and his friend Mr. Newton, traced the boy and found him. Peter Manton had a hand in the kidnapping scheme.

By the sale of the Bronx land Mrs. Dexter became possessed of enough money to put her beyond the fear of immediate want; Larry decided to continue on in the newspaper field, and when this story opens he was regarded as one of the best workers on the staff of the *Leader*. His assignment to get the story of the wreck was his first big one since the incidents told of in the second volume.

At Larry and the coast-guard trudged down the beach the guns from the doomed steamer were fired more frequently, and the rockets lighted up the darkness with a weird glare.

"Not much farther now," remarked George, as he peered ahead through the blackness, whitened here and there with masses of flying spray.

A little later they were at the life-saving station. The place was in seeming confusion, yet every man was at his post. Most of them were hauling out the long wagon frame, on which the life-boat rested. They were bringing the craft down to the beach to try to launch it.

"Lend a hand!" cried Captain Needam, as Larry and the coast-guard came in. "We need every man we can get."

Larry grasped a rope. No one paid any attention to him, and they seemed to think it was natural that he should be there. Perhaps they took him for Bailey.

The boat was taken down to the edge of the surf. An effort was made to launch it, but, struggle as the men did, they could not get it beyond the line of breakers.

"It's no use!" exclaimed the captain. "We'll have to haul her to Johnson's Cove. Maybe it isn't so rough there."

The wagon, with the boat on it, was pulled back, and then began a journey about two miles farther down the coast, to a small inlet, protected by a curving point of land. There the breakers were likely to be less high, and the boat might be launched.

Larry pulled with the rest. He did not see how he was going to get his story telegraphed to the paper, but he was consoled by the reflection that there were no other reporters on hand, and that there was no immediate likelihood of being "beaten." When morning came he could decide what to do.

So, for the time being, he became a life saver, and pulled on the long rope attached to the wagon until his arms ached. It was heavy hauling through the sand, and his feet seemed like lead.

It was nearly midnight when the cove was reached, and after a desperate struggle the life-boat was launched.

"Some of you go back and get ready to operate the breeches buoy as soon as it's light enough!" called Captain Needam, as the boat was pulled away over the heaving billows toward the wreck, which could be seen in the occasional glare of a rocket or signal light.

"Might as well come back," said George Tucker to Larry. "Can't do any more here."

Back through the wind and rain they walked, with half a score of others. They reached the life-saving station, tired and spent from their struggle through the storm.

"You can go back to Bailey," said George, as Larry sat down inside the warm and cozy living-room of the station to rest. "He may need you."

"I thought I could help here," replied Larry. "Besides, I'd like to see you work the breeches buoy."

"You'll see all you want of that in the morning," replied the coast patrol. "We can't do much until daylight. Are you afraid to go back alone?"

"No," replied Larry.

Back he trudged to Bailey's cabin. It was about three o'clock when he reached there, and he found the fisherman sitting beside the table, drinking some hot tea.

"I thought you'd got lost," spoke the fisherman.

"I went to help 'em launch the boat. They needed me. George Tucker was coming for you, but I told him of the man we saved. How is he?"

"Doing well. He's asleep in the next room. He had been struck on the head by something, and that was what made him senseless. It wasn't the water. I soon brought him around. How about the wreck?"

Larry told all he knew. Bailey insisted on the young reporter drinking two cups of steaming hot tea, and Larry felt much better after it. Then he and the fisherman stretched out on the floor to wait until morning, which would soon break.

Bailey was up early, and his movements in the hut as he shook down the fire and made coffee, aroused Larry.

"We'll get a bit of breakfast and then we'll go down to the station," said the fisherman. "I guess our man will be all right."

He went outside to bring in some wood. A moment later the door of the inner room, where the rescued man was, opened, and a head was thrust out.

"If my clothes are dry I'll take them," the man said, and Larry, glancing at him, saw that the stranger was smooth-shaven. The reporter was sure that when he was pulled from the water on the raft the man had had a heavy beard.

"Why—why—" began the youth—"your whiskers. Did you——?"

"Whiskers?" replied the man with a laugh. "Oh, you thought that bunch of seaweed on my face was a beard. I see. No, this is the way I looked. But are my clothes dry?"

Larry took them from a chair near the fire, where Bailey had hung them. He gave them to the stranger. Larry was much puzzled. It seemed as if he had stumbled upon a secret. The man shut the door of his room, A moment later the fisherman called from without the hut:

"Come on! Never mind breakfast! They're going to fire the gun!"

CHAPTER IV

RESCUED FROM THE SEA

Larry paused only long enough to don his oilskins, as it was still raining hard. The coffee was made, but he did not wait for any, though he wanted it very much. But he knew he ought to be on the spot to see all the details of the rescue from the sea, and it was not the first time he, like many other reporters, had gone on duty, and remained so for long stretches, without a meal.

Bailey was some distance down the beach. He had on his yellow suit, which he had donned to go out to the woodshed, some distance from his hut. Larry caught up to him. He was about to speak of the man at the hut when the fisherman cried:

"Something's wrong! They're coming up this way with the apparatus! Must be they couldn't find a good place down there to rig the breeches buoy."

Larry looked down the beach. He saw through the rain and mist a crowd of yellow-suited figures approaching, dragging something along the sand. He looked out to sea and beheld the blotch that represented the doomed vessel. All thought of the man at the hut was, for the time, driven out of his mind.

On came the life savers. They halted about a mile from the hut, and Larry and Bailey ran to join them.

"Did you save any?" called the fisherman to Captain Needam, who was busy directing the rescue.

"Got some in the life-boat early this morning," was the answer. "They took 'em to the lower station. We couldn't get back with the boat. All ready now, men. Dig a hole for the anchor, Nate. Sam, you help plant the mortar. Have to allow a good bit for the wind. My! but she's blowin' great guns and little pistols!"

Larry had his first sight of a rescue by means of the breeches buoy. The apparatus, including a small cannon or mortar, had been brought from the life-saving station on a wagon, pulled by the men along the beach. The first act was to dig a deep hole in the sand, some distance back from the surf. This was to hold the anchor, to which was attached the shore end of the heavy rope, on which, presently, persons from the wreck might be hauled ashore.

Once the anchor was in the hole, and covered with sand, firmly packed down, arrangements were made to get a line to the vessel.

"Put in a heavy charge!" cried Captain Needam. "We'll need lots of powder to get the shot aboard in the teeth of this wind!"

Several men grouped about the brass cannon and rapidly loaded the weapon. Then, instead of a cannon ball, they put in a long, solid piece of iron, shaped like the modern shell, with a pointed nose. To this projectile was attached a long, thin, but very strong line.

"Are they going to fire that at the ship?" asked Larry, who was not very familiar with nautical matters.

"They hope to have it land right on deck, or carry the line over," said Bailey, who paused in his work of helping the men to lay out from the wagon parts of the apparatus.

Larry watched intently. Now and then he gazed out to the ship, a speck of black amid white foam, for the seas were breaking over her.

At the side of the cannon was a box, containing the line, one end of which was fastened to the projectile. The rope was coiled in a peculiar cris-cross manner, to prevent it being tangled as it paid rapidly out when the shot was fired.

"All ready?" called Captain Needam, as he looked at his men.

"Ready, sir," answered George Tucker.

"Put in the primer!" ordered the chief of the life savers. One of the men inserted a percussion fuse in the touchhole of the mortar. The captain grasped a lanyard. The men all stood at attention, waiting to see the effect of the shot.

Captain Needam sighted over the muzzle of the cannon. It was pointed so as to clear the stern of the ship, but this was necessary, as the high wind would carry the projectile to one side.

The arm of the captain stiffened. The lanyard tauted. There was a spark at the breach of the mortar, a sharp crackle as the primer ignited, and then a dull boom as the charge was fired. Through the mist of rain Larry saw a black object shooting out toward the ship. After it trailed the long thin line, like a tail to a kite.

It was scarcely a moment later that there sounded a gun from the ship.

"Good!" cried Captain Needam. "The shot went true!"

"That was the ship signalling that they had the line," explained Bailey, shouting the words in Larry's ear.

From the shore to the ship there now stretched out a long thin rope. Larry had no time to wonder what would happen next.

"Bend on the cable!" cried the captain, and the men quickly attached a thick rope to the line which the cannon-shot had carried aboard the *Olivia*. This soon began to pay out, as it was hauled in by those on the wrecked vessel. In a short time the heavy cable was all out, and securely fastened to the ship, high enough up so as to clear the rail. Directions how to do this were printed on a board which was hauled in with the rope, and, lest those on a doomed ship might not understand English, the instructions were given in several languages.

"They have it fast! Rig up the shears!" cried the captain.

Once more his men were busy. They set up on the sand two stout wooden pieces, exactly like, a pair of enormous shears. The longer parts, corresponding to the blades, were nearest the ground, while what answered for the handles were several feet in the air, opened in "V" shape.

Through this "V" the heavy cable was passed, the one end being fast to the anchor buried in the sand, and the other being attached to the ship. By moving the shears nearer to the anchor the cable was tightened until it hung taut from shore to ship, a slender bridge on which to save life.

The breeches buoy, a canvas arrangement, shaped like a short pair of trousers, and attached to a frame which ran back and forth on the cable by means of pulleys, had been adjusted. To it were fastened ropes, one being retained by the life savers and one by those on the ship. All was in readiness.

The breeches buoy was now pulled toward the ship, by those aboard hauling on the proper line. It moved along, sliding on the heavy cable, the angry waves below seeming to try to leap up and engulf it, in revenge for being cheated of their prey.

"Look sharp now, men!" cried the captain. "Get ready to take care of the poor souls as they come ashore."

The storm still kept up, and the waves were so high that a second attempt to save some by means of the life-boat, even launching it in the protected cove, had to be given up. But the breeches buoy could be depended on.

A signal from the ship told those on shore that the buoy was loaded with a passenger, and ready to be hauled back. Willing hands pulled on the rope. On it came through the driving rain; on it came above the waves, though not so high but what the spray from the crests wet the rescued one.

"It's a woman!" cried the captain, as he caught sight of the person in the buoy.

"And a baby! Bless my soul!" added Bailey. "She's got a baby in her arms!"

And so it proved; for, wrapped in a shawl, which was tied over her shoulders, so as to keep the water from the tiny form, was an infant clasped tightly to its mother's breast.

"Take her to the station!" cried the captain, as he helped the woman to get out of the canvas holder in which she had ridden safely to shore. "My wife will look after her. Now for the rest, men. There's lots of 'em, and the ship can't last much longer! Lively, men. Every minute means a life!"

"I'll take her to the station!" volunteered Larry, for there was nothing he could do to help now, and he thought he could get a good story of the wreck from the first person rescued.

"Go ahead!" exclaimed the life savers' captain.

The woman, in spite of her terrible experience, had not fainted. Still clasping her baby, she moved through the crowd of men, who cheered her as they set to work again.

"Come with me," said Larry. "We will take care of you!"

"Oh, it is so good to be on land again!" the woman cried. "I am not a coward— but oh, the cruel waves!" and she shuddered.

CHAPTER V

LARRY'S SCOOP

"Are there many women aboard?" asked Larry, as he moved off through the rain toward the life-saving station with the rescued passenger.

"I was the only one," was the answer the woman made, in a pronounced Italian accent. "I am the purser's wife. They made me come first. Me and the baby," and she put her lips down and kissed the little face nestled in the folds of the shawl.

"The purser's wife!" exclaimed Larry. "Perhaps your husband will bring the passenger list with him. I would like to get it. I am a newspaper reporter," he added.

The woman, with a rapid movement, held out a bundle of papers to him.

"What are they?" Larry asked.

"The list of passengers! You reporters! I have heard of you in my country, but they do not such things as this! Go to wrecks to meet the passengers when they come ashore! You are very brave!"

"I think you were brave to come first across the waves," replied Larry. "The rope might break."

"I had my baby," was the answer, as if that explained it all.

"Do you think your husband would let me telegraph these names to my paper?" asked Larry.

"He gave them to me to bring ashore, in case—in case the ship did not last," the purser's wife said, with a catch in her voice. "You may use them, I say so. I will make it right."

This was just what Larry wanted. The hardest things to get in an accident or a wreck are the names of the saved, or the dead and injured. Chance had placed in Larry's hands just what he wanted.

He hurried on with the woman, who told him her name was Mrs. Angelino. He did not question her further, as he felt she must be suffering from the strain she had undergone. In a short time they were safe at the station, and there Mrs.

Needam provided warm and dry garments for mother and child, and gave Mrs. Angelino hot drinks.

"Ah, there is my reporter!" exclaimed the purser's wife, when she was warm and comfortable, as she saw Larry busy scanning the list of passengers. "He came quick to the wreck!"

"Can you lend me some paper?" Larry asked Mrs. Needam.

"What for?"

"I want to write an account of the rescue and copy these names. I must hurry to the telegraph office. I left my paper in the fisherman's hut."

"I'll get you some," said Captain Needam's wife, and soon Larry was writing a short but vivid story of what had taken place, including a description of the storm, and the saving of the only woman on board, with her baby, by means of the breeches buoy. Then he copied the list of names.

"There's something I almost forgot," said Larry when he had about finished. "There's that passenger who came ashore on the life-raft. I wonder who he was? I'll ask Mrs. Angelino."

But she did not know. She was not aware that any one had come ashore on a raft, for, in the confusion of the breaking up of the ship in the storm, she thought only of her husband, her baby and herself.

"I can find out later," Larry thought.

He gave the list back to Mrs. Angelino, and then, with a good preliminary story of the wreck, having obtained many facts from the purser's wife, Larry set out through the storm for the nearest telegraph station.

"Don't you want some hot coffee before you go?" asked Mrs. Needam. "I've got lots—ready for the poor souls that'll soon be here."

Larry did want some. He was conscious of a woeful lack of something in his stomach, and the coffee braced him up in a way he very much needed.

It was quite a distance from the life-saving station to the nearest telegraph office, but Larry knew he must make it if he wanted an account of the wreck to get to his paper in time for the edition that day. So he set off for a tiresome trudge over the wet sand. As he was leaving, several men, who had been brought ashore from the ship, came to the station. From them Larry learned that part of the ship was likely to last until all the passengers and crew could be saved. He then resolved to telegraph the story of the saving of all, knowing he could make corrections by an additional message later in case, by some accident, any lives were lost.

To get to the telegraph office Larry had to go back to a point nearly opposite where the life savers were working, and then strike inland. As he was hurrying along he came to a little hummock of sand, from which elevation he could look down on the beach and see the crowd gathered about the breeches buoy. Out on the bar he could make out the wrecked vessel. As he stood there a moment he saw some one detach himself from the crowd and hurry across the intervening beach.

"That figure looks familiar," thought Larry. "I wonder if that's Bailey the fisherman?"

He waited a few minutes, and the figure became more distinct.

"It's Peter Manton!" cried Larry. "He's been sent down here to report the wreck! I wonder what paper he's on? But I guess I haven't any time to stand here wondering. I've got to beat him to the telegraph office if I want to get a scoop, though he can't have been on hand long enough to get much of an account."

Still Larry knew that even a brief and poor account of anything, if it got in first, was enough to discount or "take the edge off" a better story told later, and he made up his mind he would "scoop" Peter, his old enemy.

The representative of the *Leader* hurried on. Peter caught sight of Larry, and recognized him in spite of his oilskins. Peter wore a rain-coat, which was wet through.

"Hold on, Larry!" he cried. "I'm on the *Scorcher* again. What have you got?"

It was the newspaper man's way of asking his brother-of-the-pencil for such information as he possessed. But though, as a general thing, when several reporters are on a general story, they interchange common news, Larry was in no mind to share what he had with Peter. His paper had gone to the trouble to send him down in good season, a piece of forethought which the other journals' editors had neglected. Therefor Larry felt that he was not violating the common practice (though it is against the strict office rules) if he ignored Peter.

"Haven't time!" he called back.

"Wait a minute!" cried the rival reporter. "I just came down on the first train, and I walked about five miles to find the wreck. I'm going to the telegraph office to send my account in for an extra. We'll whack up on it."

"We'll do nothing of the sort!" exclaimed Larry. "I don't want anything to do with you." He had never forgiven Peter for his part in the kidnapping of Jimmie.

"Needn't get huffy about it," remarked Peter. "I want to be friendly."

Larry thought it was hardly Peter's place to offer to be "friendly" after the mean part he had played.

"I haven't time to stop now," said Larry. "I'm in a hurry. You'll have to get along the best you can."

"So that's how you feel, eh?" asked the rival reporter. "Not very white of you, Larry Dexter. I've only just got back my job on the *Scorcher* after they laid me off for getting beaten, and I've got to make good. But never mind. The beach is free, and I've got as good a right to the telegraph office as you have. I'd like to see you beat me."

Larry himself did not just see how he would, but he made up his mind to attempt it. Peter was now keeping pace with him. There was nothing for it but to hurry on. Whoever reached the office first and "filed his copy" would have the right to the wire. Larry resolved that he would win in the race, even as he had won in the other, at the big flood, but he knew there was time enough yet. If he started to run Peter would run also, and the way was too long for a fast sprint.

The two kept on, side by side, neither speaking. The only sound was the patter of the rain, and the rustle and rattle of Larry's oilskin suit.

They passed through the deserted summer resort. It was about a mile now to the telegraph office. Larry recalled that Bailey had told him there was a short cut by keeping to the railroad track, and he turned into that highway, followed by Peter, who, it seemed, had resolved not to lose sight of his rival.

It was now about nine o'clock, though his activity since early morning made it seem much later to Larry. He knew he had a good story safe in his pocket, and he was pretty sure Peter had only a garbled account, for he could not have gotten the facts so quickly. Nor did he, Larry was sure, have the passenger list, which was the best part of the story.

On and on the two rivals trudged silently. They must be near the office now, Larry thought, and he looked ahead through the rain. They were in the midst of a little settlement of fishermen's houses—a small village—but it was nearly deserted, as most of the inhabitants had gone to the wreck. Larry saw a building on which was a sign informing those who cared to know that it contained a store, the post-office and a place whence telegrams might be sent and received. Peter saw it at the same instant.

"Here's where I beat you!" he cried as he sprang forward on the run.

Larry tried to follow, but his legs became entangled in the oilskin coat and he fell. He was up again in an instant, only to see Peter entering the office. Larry's heart seemed like lead. Had he worked so hard only to be beaten at the last?

Something spurred him on. He stumbled into the office in time to hear Peter saying:

"I want to hold a wire for a long despatch to the New York *Scorcher*. I've got a big account of the wreck."

"Where's your copy?" asked the young man in charge of the clicking instruments.

"I'll have it ready for you in a minute," replied Peter, sitting down to a table, and beginning to dash off words and sentences as fast as his pencil could fly.

"I can't hold any wire for you," said the operator. "If you have any press stuff to file let me have it. That's the only way you can keep a wire."

"I'll have it for you in a second," Peter replied as he looked anxiously at the door.

"That will not answer. I must have copy in order to keep the wire busy."

"Here it is!" cried Larry, as he entered at that moment and pulled from his pocket his hastily written account of the wreck, including the list of passengers. "I'll be obliged to you if you canget this off to the New York *Leader* as soon as possible."

"I was here first!" angrily cried Peter.

"But I have his copy first," the operator said. "It is the filing of the despatch first that counts, not who gets here first. I'll get this off right away for you," he added, turning to Larry.

And thus it was that Larry got his scoop, for his account took so long to telegraph that, when the operator began on Peter's, the *Leader* had the story in the office, and was preparing to get out an extra.

CHAPTER VI

A STRANGE DISAPPEARANCE

Remaining only long enough to see that the operator got off the first part of his story, and finding, on inquiry, that the telegrapher had no difficulty in reading his writing, Larry started back to the scene of the wreck. He wanted to learn if all the passengers and crew were saved, and get an interview with the captain, if he could.

So he left his old enemy, Peter, there grinding out his story in no pleasant frame of mind. But it was part of the game, and Larry's "beat" was a cleanly-scored one, especially as Peter had tried to win by a trick.

The young reporter found the work of rescue almost completed. The life savers had labored to good advantage and had brought nearly all the passengers ashore in the breeches buoy. They were cared for temporarily at the beach station, though the small quarters were hardly adequate.

With the bringing ashore of the crew and officers, the captain coming last, the life savers found their work finished. And it was only just in time, for, not more than an hour after the commander had staggered up the beach, worn and exhausted by the strain and exposure, the after part of the vessel slid from the bar and sank in deep water.

Larry, who had been introduced to Captain Needam by Bailey, told the former of his desire for an interview with the commander of the *Olivia*, and the matter was soon arranged, though Captain Tantrella was in dire distress over the loss of his ship.

However, he told Larry what the reporter wished to know, describing how, in the fog, the vessel had run on the sand bar. He related some of the scenes during their wait to be rescued, told of the high seas and terrible winds, and painted a vivid picture of the dangers. Larry wrote it in his best style and hurried back to the telegraph office.

There was only one passenger missing, and the name of this one, according to the purser's list, was Mah Retto. The name, though peculiar, Larry thought, was not dissimilar to scores of others, for the steamer had on board a cosmopolitan lot of passengers. No one knew how Retto had been lost.

As Larry was on his way to the telegraph office a sudden thought came to him.

"That's it!" he exclaimed. "The man who came ashore on the life-raft is this missing Mah Retto. I'll just stop on my way to the telegraph office and see him. That will clear it all up, and make every passenger accounted for."

He hurried on, intending to get a hasty interview with the man at Bailey's hut, and then go telegraph the rest of his story. The fisherman was still down on the beach, aiding the life savers to pack their apparatus for transportation back to the station. As Larry came in sight of the cabin he saw the raft, on which the stranger had come ashore, lying just beyond high-water mark.

He entered the hut, expecting to see Retto, as he had come to call the foreigner, sitting comfortably by the fire. But the rescued man was not there. Nor was he in the room where he had been put to bed.

"Maybe he's in the woodshed," thought Larry. "I'll take a look."

But he was not there.

"That's strange," Larry mused. "He's disappeared. There is something queer in this, and I'm going to find it out. But first I must send the rest of my story."

Larry found Peter Manton still at the telegraph office grinding away. Larry's first batch of copy had been sent off, as had most of Peter's stuff. As the representative of the *Scorcher* handed in the last of his copy he turned to Larry and said, sneeringly:

"I'll bet I've got a better story than you have."

"Perhaps," was all Larry replied. Then, as Peter went back to the wreck for more information, Larry wrote, as an addition to his story, the interview with the captain, finishing with an account of the missing Mah Retto. He told also of the man who came ashore on the raft, and who was believed to be the passenger who was unaccounted for.

"That's a good day's work done," remarked the young reporter, as he signed his name to the last sheet of copy. "I wonder if they want me to stay here?"

He wrote a brief message asking Mr. Emberg for instructions. Telling the operator he would call in about two hours for an answer, Larry decided he would get some breakfast.

As there was no restaurant in the little hamlet, he thought the best plan would be to go back to the fisherman's cabin. He wanted to talk with Bailey about the disappearance of the man they had rescued from the raft.

The fisherman was at the hut when Larry arrived, and was busy preparing a meal.

"Guess you feel like eating something, don't ye?" he asked.

"You guessed it right the first time," replied the young reporter, with a grin.

"And my other company," went on Bailey. "I expect he's hungry."

"He's gone."

"Gone?"

"Yes; I came back here a while ago and there wasn't a sign of him."

"Why, that's queer," returned the fisherman. "I've been so busy frying this bacon and making fresh coffee I didn't notice it. But that reminds me, I haven't seen or heard anything of him since I came in. His clothes are gone, too."

Larry and Bailey made a hasty search through the cabin. There were few places where a person could conceal himself, and they very soon found that their late guest was nowhere on the premises.

"Here's something," remarked Larry, as he looked on a small table in the room where the rescued man had slept. "It looks like a note."

It was a note, written on the fly leaf torn from a book. It read:

"Dear friends. Accept my thanks for saving my life. Please take this small remembrance for your trouble."

There was no signature to the note, but folded in the paper was a hundred-dollar bill, somewhat damp from immersion in the sea.

"Well, sink my cuttle-fish!" exclaimed Bailey. "That's odd. A hundred dollars! That's more than I make in a summer season. But half of it's yours. I'd like to rescue people steady at that rate."

"It's all yours," said Larry. "I got the story I came down after, and that's all I want. But I would like to find this Mah Retto, if that's his name. He doesn't write much like a foreigner, though he looks like one. May I keep this note?"

"As long as you don't want a share in the hundred-dollar one, I reckon you can," Bailey replied, with a laugh.

Larry folded the scrap of paper to put in his pocket. As he did so something bright and shining on the floor attracted his attention. He stooped to pick it up, finding it was a small gold coin, of curious design, evidently used as a watch charm.

"I guess our man dropped this," Larry said, holding it out to Bailey.

"Well, you can keep that, with the note. Perhaps it will help you solve the mystery," the fisherman said. "I'm satisfied with what I got."

Larry put the charm in his pocket, together with the note, and was about to leave the room, when the fisherman, who was lifting from the corner a box, in which to deposit his money, uttered an exclamation.

"What is it?" asked Larry.

"Why, it's a man's beard. Somebody's shaved his off and left it here. How in the name of a soft-shell clam——"

"It's that man!" cried Larry. "I knew he had a beard on when we pulled him ashore!"

"A beard on?" murmured Bailey, in questioning tones.

"Yes," went on Larry. "When you were outside, getting some wood, just before you ran down the beach when the life savers came, I was in here. The man stuck his head from the bed-room and asked for his clothes, which I gave him. I noticed he was smooth shaven——"

"Why, he had a beard on when we pulled him from the water," interrupted the fisherman.

"I was sure he did, but when I asked him why he had shaved it off he said I was mistaken—said it was only a bunch of seaweed I had thought was a beard. Then you called me to hurry out, and I forgot all about it until now. But he must have shaved his whiskers off in here, and then he disappeared. There's something strange about it all."

"I rather guess there is," Bailey admitted. "Wonder where he got his razor? I never use one."

"He must have had it in that small valise he wore, strapped by a belt, around his waist," Larry answered. "That's probably where he carried his money. I'd like to get at the bottom of this mystery."

"Well, you newspaper fellows are looking for just such things as this," said the fisherman with a smile. "It's right in your line."

"So it is," Larry replied. "I'll solve it, too."

But it was some time later, and Larry had many strange adventures before he got at the bottom of the queer secret that started down there on the lonely sea coast.

CHAPTER VII

LARRY OVERHEARS SOMETHING

Larry decided that the disappearance of the fisherman's guest was not a part of the story of the wreck, though the fact that the passenger was missing was an item of much interest, and he used it. He made up his mind to tell Mr. Emberg all about the strange happening when he got back.

Arriving at the telegraph office for the third time, he found a message from the city editor, instructing him to come back to New York, as the best of the story was now in, and the Associated Press would attend to the remainder. Some of the representatives of that news-gathering organization were already at the scene of the disaster.

"Your friend got a calling down," volunteered the operator to Larry, as the young reporter began looking up trains to see when he could get back.

"How's that?"

"He got a message from his city editor a while ago, wanting to know why he hadn't secured a list of passengers and the crew. The message said the *Leader* had it, and had beaten all the other papers."

"That's good," spoke Larry. "I worked hard enough for it."

"The *Scorcher* man wanted me to give him your list, but I wouldn't do it," the operator went on. "So he's gone out to get one of his own. But he's too late, I reckon. I'll have my hands full pretty soon, for there'll be a lot of reporters here. But you're the first to send off the complete story."

Larry felt much elated. Of course he knew it was due, in part, to the forethought of his city editor in seeing a possible situation, and rushing a man to the scene ahead of the other papers. That counts for almost as much in journalism as does getting a good story or a "scoop."

Larry received hearty congratulations from Mr. Emberg when he got back to the *Leader* office the next day, for, not only had the young reporter secured a fine "scoop," but he had sent in an exceptionally good story of the wreck.

"Larry, you did better than I thought you would. You've got the right stuff in you!" exclaimed the city editor, while the other reporters, crowding around the hero of the occasion, expressed, their pleasure at his success. Not one of them but would have given much to have been in Larry's place.

"Have much trouble?" asked Mr. Newton.

"Well, I had to hustle. Struck something rather queer down there, too."

"What was it? Some of the men from other papers try to get the best of you?"

"Only my old enemy, Peter Manton, but I put a crimp in him all right. No, this was something else." And Larry told of the disappearance of the man at the hut.

"That is rather odd," agreed the older reporter. "If I were you I'd tell Mr. Emberg about it, and then you'll be in a position to act on what information you have, in case anything turns up."

Larry followed this advice. The city editor puzzled over the matter a few minutes, and then decided nothing could be done at present.

"We'll watch developments in regard to the *Olivia* wreck," said Mr. Emberg, "and it may be this mystery will fit in somewhere. If it does we may get a good story."

But neither Larry nor the city editor realized in what a strange manner the mystery was to develop.

It was the beginning of the newspaper day in the *Leader* office. Reporters were busy writing accounts of meetings they had covered the previous night, and others were going out on assignments to police courts, to look up robberies, murders, suicides, and the hundred and one things that go to make up the news of the day.

"How would you like to try your hand at politics?" asked Mr. Emberg of Larry, when they had finished their talk about the man at the hut. "I haven't given you much chance at anything in that line, but if you're going to be an all-'round newspaper man you'll have a lot to do with politics."

"I think I'd like it," replied Larry.

Certainly this life was one of variety, one day at the wild scene of a rescue from a wreck, and the next peacefully sent to talk to some political leader.

"I want you to go up and have a talk with Jack Sullivan, the leader of one of the Assembly districts," went on Mr. Emberg. "You've probably read of the trouble in that district. Thomas Kilburn is a new aspirant for the Assembly and he's fighting against the re-nomination of William Reilly. Now Jack Sullivan is the leader of that district, and whoever he decides to support will be elected. That's the way politics are run in New York.

"It would be quite an item of news if we could find out whom Sullivan is going to support. So far he has played foxy and no one knows, not even the candidates themselves, I believe, though I have an idea that Sullivan will swing to Reilly."

"How did Kilburn come to be in the race?" asked Larry.

"That's what we newspaper editors would like to know, and it's what you reporters have to find out for us. There's something back of it all. Sullivan wants something he thinks either Kilburn or Reilly can give him, and that's why he's holding back. He'll give his support to the man who, after he's elected, can give him what he wants. Now if you could discover whom Sullivan is going to support, and why, it would make a corking story."

"I'll try," said Larry, a little doubtful of his ability.

"It isn't at all like going down to a wreck and seeing persons rescued," went on Mr. Emberg. "You've got to nose out your news this time. A number of reporters have tried to pump Sullivan, but he won't give up. Go and try your luck. You'll find him in the district headquarters," and he gave Larry the address.

"Where you going?" asked Mr. Newton, as he passed Larry in the corridor.

"To interview Sullivan."

Mr. Newton whistled.

"I don't envy you," he said. "I'm afraid you'll fall down this time, Larry" ("falling-down" being a newspaper man's term for failure). "We've all tried him, but he's as cute as an old fox. He'll be nice and polite, but he'll not give you a decided answer, one way or the other."

"I've got to try," was Larry's reply.

Larry had one advantage on his side. He was a new reporter in the political field. That was one reason why Mr. Emberg sent him. Nearly all the other available men on the *Leader* were well known to the politicians, they were familiar with them, and, as soon as they saw these reporters, the politicians were on their guard.

Larry, never before having talked with Sullivan and his friends, might take them off their guard, and they might let fall something that would make news, the city editor thought. It was a slim chance, but newspaper editors are accustomed to taking such.

When Larry entered the headquarters of Sullivan, which were located in the rear of a large dance hall, he found the place well filled with men, though it was the middle of the forenoon, when most persons would have been at work. But the men were politicians of more or less power, and had plenty of spare time. Besides this was really their work, though it did not look like very strenuous labor, for most of them were standing in little groups, talking and smoking, or sitting in chairs tilted back against the wall.

Here was where Larry's newness gave him an advantage. No one in the room knew him to be a reporter, or he would have been greeted by some of the men as soon as he entered, called by name, and thus all the others would have been put on their guard.

Larry sauntered into the big room as though he belonged there. He hardly knew what to do, but he decided to look about for a few minutes and size up the situation. No one paid any attention to him, and he felt it would be a good plan to see if he could pick Sullivan out from among the throng.

With this end in view Larry walked from one end of the room to the other. He did not know that the man he sought was in his private office, closeted with some of his henchmen. As Larry passed one group he heard one man in it say:

"Well, Sullivan's made up his mind at last."

"He has, eh?" asked another. "Who is it?"

Larry was all attention at once. This seemed to be the very thing he had been sent to find out.

"Don't let it get out," went on the man who had first spoken, "but I understand Tommy has got to wait a while yet."

"Then Billy can probably deliver the goods," the second man added. "I thought he could. Well, it means a good thing for the district when they build the new line. If only Potter doesn't go back on his promise. He's so rich you can't touch him with money, and he's as foxy as they make 'em. If Billy can work him I don't blame Sullivan for swinging his way. Now——"

But at that moment one of the men turned and saw Larry. He at once knew him for a stranger, and quickly inquired:

"What do you want, young man?"

"I want to see Mr. Sullivan."

Larry didn't announce himself as a reporter, for that, he felt, would have brought him only a polite refusal, on Sullivan's part, to receive him.

"What for?" went on the man.

"I have a message for him," Larry said.

"You can tell me, I'll see that he gets it."

"It is for him personally," Larry said, for a bold plan had come into his mind and he determined to try it.

CHAPTER VIII

AN INTERVIEW WITH SULLIVAN

For a moment the man who had questioned Larry stood gazing at him. Suspicion was in the look, but the reporter never quailed. He was playing a bold game and he was running a risk, but he was not going to give up so soon.

"What's your name?" the man asked him.

"Larry Dexter."

That conveyed nothing to his questioner, for Larry had not been long enough on the *Leader* to become known in the field of politics. There were some men in the newspaper business with whom the politicians were so familiar that they sent for them whenever they had any news they were desirous of making public. But Larry was not yet one of these.

"Sam, tell Mr. Sullivan a young man wants to see him personally," went on the man who had interrogated Larry. "You can take a seat over there," he added, pointing to some chairs farthest removed from the group of which he was a member.

As Larry moved away he heard one of the men remark:

"Wonder if he's a newspaper man?"

"I don't believe so," replied another. "I've never seen him before and I know most of the reporters in New York. None of the editors would send a new man to interview Sullivan. He's too tough a bird for a greenhorn to tackle. I guess he's a messenger from some broker's office. Maybe Potter sent him."

"I wonder who this Potter is, and what all that talk meant?" Larry thought to himself as he took a chair, and watched the messenger enter a small room at the end of the big apartment.

In a little while Sam, who appeared to be a sort of janitor around the place, came back to inform Larry that Sullivan would see him.

"Now for my game of bluff," said the young reporter to himself as he entered.

The political leader was sitting behind a desk, littered with papers. He was a small man, wearing glasses, and looking like anything but the chief factor of an important Assembly district. Mr. Sullivan was bald-headed, and had rather a pleasant face, but there was a look about him that indicated force of character, of a certain kind, and a determination to succeed in what he undertook, which is what makes a good politician.

"You wanted to see me?" and the question came in a low voice, totally unlike the loud tones Larry had, somehow, associated with an important politician.

Larry felt the eyes of Sullivan gazing sharply at him, as though they were sizing him up, labeling him, and placing him on a certain shelf to be kept there until wanted. Sullivan was a good reader of character, as he showed by his next question.

"What paper are you from?"

Larry started. He wondered how the man knew he was from a paper, for Larry had said nothing about it. Seeing his confusion Sullivan laughed.

"Wondering how I took your measure, aren't you?" he asked, and when Larry nodded he went on: "You have the air of a newspaper man, which you may consider flattering, as you have acquired it after having been in the game only a short time. I assume that because it's my business to know most of the reporters in this city, and I never saw you before. If you didn't look like a newspaper man I'd size you up for one, because only a reporter, or some of my political friends, would come here to see me. You're not the one, so you must be the other. Now what do you want?" and the politician's voice became rather sharp.

"I came here to find out if it's true that you're going to support Reilly because he can deliver the goods from Mr. Potter," Larry explained, resolving to chance all at once.

Sullivan started, and half arose from his chair. Then he seemed to recover himself.

"Some one's been talking!" he murmured, and, glancing quickly at Larry, he asked:

"Who is Mr. Potter? I'm afraid I don't understand you."

"He's the financier interested in the new line," went on Larry, boldly. "It's going to be a good thing for the district, I understand. Come now, Mr. Sullivan," he went on, assuming a familiar air he did not feel, "you might as well own up and give me an interview about deciding to support Reilly."

For several seconds the leader gazed at Larry, as if seeking to read his inmost thoughts. Then he spoke:

"You either know too much or too little, Dexter. I guess you're an older hand at this business than I took you for. Tell me what you know."

"You tell me what I want to know," Larry said with a smile. "You probably know all that I do and more, too. But I don't know half as much as you do about this, though I know enough to print something in the *Leader*. You might as well come out with it."

Sullivan hesitated. He was wondering how this new young reporter had discovered information supposed to be a secret among the politician's closest advisers. Clearly there was a leak somewhere, and he must play the game warily until he discovered it. Meanwhile, since part of the truth was known he decided to tell more of it. He could manage matters to suit his ends if necessary, even after he gave out the interview for which all the papers in New York were anxiously waiting.

"Did Mr. Emberg send you to see me?" asked Sullivan.

"He did," Larry answered, wondering how intimate was the politician's acquaintance with the city editor of the *Leader*.

"Emberg's foxy," went on Sullivan.

"Do I get the interview?" asked Larry.

"You do. I like your nerve, and I'd like to find out where you heard that about Potter."

Larry did not think it well to say he had merely overheard, in the politician's own headquarters, a reference to the man, who was a well-known millionaire and promoter of New York. The truth of the matter was Larry only used the information that had so unexpectedly come to him, but he used it in such a way that Sullivan thought he knew a great deal more than he did.

"I'm going to support Reilly," went on Sullivan. "I don't know that I have such great influence as the papers credit me with, but what I have is for my friend,

William Reilly. You can say for me that I think he served well in the Legislature and is entitled to another term. As for Mr. Kilburn, who I hear would like the nomination, he is an excellent young man. I know little about him, but I believe he would do well. But I believe in rewarding good work, and so I am for Mr. Reilly."

"Do you want to say anything about Potter and the new line?" asked Larry, though if Sullivan had said anything about them the reporter would have been decidedly in the dark as to what the politician was driving at.

"I guess you've got enough out of me for one day," replied Sullivan with a smile. "It's more talking than I've done in a long while—to reporters," he added. "Lots of 'em would give a good bit to have what you've got, and I wouldn't have given it to you, only I think you're smarter than I gave you credit for. Now you tell me where you heard about Potter."

"I can't," answered Larry, truthfully enough, for he did not feel that he could betray one of Sullivan's own men, because of the talk he had inadvertently overheard. "Sometime I may."

"I'll have to cultivate your acquaintance," the district politician remarked as Larry went out.

The young reporter hurried to the *Leader* office, having hastily jotted down what Sullivan had said. He felt he had secured a piece of news that would prove a big item that day.

"What luck?" asked Mr. Emberg, rather indifferently, as Larry came up to the city editor's desk to report.

"I've got the interview."

"I s'pose he gave you a lot of hot air that doesn't mean anything. See if you can dress it up a bit. We haven't many displays to-day."

"Sullivan is going to support Reilly," announced Larry, quietly.

"What?" almost shouted Mr. Emberg. "Did he tell you that?"

"He did," answered Larry, wondering why Mr. Emberg was so excited.

CHAPTER IX

EVERYTHING BUT THE FACTS

The city room, that had been buzzing and humming with the talk of several reporters, seemed strangely quiet as Larry gave his answer. His remarks had been heard by several. The clicking typewriters stopped, and those operating them looked up.

"Say that again," spoke Mr. Emberg, as though a great deal depended on it.

"Sullivan is going to support Reilly," repeated Larry. "There's what he says," and he handed out the brief interview which he had written on some sheets of paper as he came down in the elevated train. The city editor glanced quickly over it.

"Are you sure you haven't made a mistake?" he asked.

"I'm positive that's exactly what he said."

"This is a big thing," went on Mr. Emberg. "We have news from Albany directly contrary to this, but if you're sure you are right I'll use this. It will make a big sensation. Have you got it all alone?"

"There were no other reporters there that I knew," Larry said.

"Good for you. How in the world did you do it? I never thought you would. Sit right down and make as much as you can of it. Describe how he received you, what you said and what he said and all about it. This is great."

"I stumbled on it," said Larry, and he proceeded to relate what he had heard about Potter and the new line, though he did not in the least know what the "new line" was.

"Better and better!" exclaimed Mr. Emberg. "This is what I suspected. It has to do with the new subway line. If it runs through the eighth district it will be the making of Sullivan. That's why he's supporting Reilly, because he thinks Reilly can influence Potter to run the new subway line in that direction. We must have an interview with Potter. I'll send some one else out on that. You write what you have. Here, Mr. Newton, jump out and see if you can find Potter. It's going to be quite a job, but maybe you can land him."

"Hamden Potter's in Europe," said a reporter who "did" Wall Street, and who knew the movements of most of the financiers. "But he's expected back soon."

"Maybe he's back by this time," Mr. Emberg went on. "Get out on the job, Newton. Hurry, Larry, it's close to edition-time."

Larry sat down at his typewriter, which he had learned to operate with considerable speed, and was soon banging away at the keys.

"Shall I put in that about Mr. Potter and the new line?" he called to Mr. Emberg.

"No, I'll have Harvey attend to that part. You just tell of the interview in regard to supporting Reilly. Make it a good story."

Larry did his best, and gave a graphic picture of the leader's headquarters, without touching on how he had come to get the information which so many other papers and reporters were anxiously waiting for.

"Here, Tommy!" called the city editor to one of the copy boys, which position Larry used to fill, "bring me Mr. Dexter's stuff, page by page, as fast as he writes it. I'll get it upstairs and fix up a head for it."

Larry smiled to hear Mr. Emberg call him "Mr. Dexter," but, no matter how familiar an editor may become with his reporters, he gives even the youngest the title of mister when speaking of him to the copy boys.

Larry finished the first page of his story, pulled it from the typewriter and handed it to Tommy, who rushed with it to Mr. Emberg's desk. The editor glanced over it, made one or two corrections, changed the wording a bit, and handed it back to Tommy, who hurried with it to the pneumatic tube, in which it was shot upstairs to the composing room.

There it was taken from the metal carrier that dropped from the tube on the desk of the man in charge of distributing the various pieces of copy to the compositors. This man put a mysterious-looking blue mark on the first page of Larry's story. This was to identify it later, and to make sure that all the succeeding pages would be kept together.

Then the sheet was handed to the first of a long line of compositors, who were standing in front of the desk of the "copy-cutter," as he is called. It was close to the hour for the first edition to go to press, and every one was in a hurry.

The compositor fairly ran to his type-setting machine and began to operate the keys, which were arranged like those on a very large typewriter. He did not strike them, as one does who operates a typewriter, but gently touched them. As he pressed each finger down the least bit there was a click, and from the rack above the machine there tumbled down a small piece of brass, called a "matrix." This contained on one edge a depression that corresponded to a letter.

In a short while enough matrixes had fallen into place to make a complete line, just the width of one of the columns of the *Leader*. The compositor looked at the row of matrixes as they were, arranged before him, read it (no easy task to the uninitiated), took out a wrong letter and inserted a right one, and then pressed down a lever.

This lever operated the lead-casting machine at the back. A plunger was shoved down into a pot of melted lead, kept molten by means of a gas flame. A small quantity of lead was forced up against the line of matrixes, which automatically moved in a position to receive it.

The lead was held there an instant to harden, then another lever automatically removed the solid line of type from its place in front of the matrixes, a long arm swooped down, took the brass pieces and returned them to an endless screw arrangement which distributed them, each one to its proper place, in the series of chutes that held hundreds of others.

Everything was done automatically after the compositor had touched the keys and then the lever, so that he was almost finished with the second line of the story by the time the matrixes of the first were being returned to their slots by the machine, which seemed almost human.

Thus Larry's story was set up. In all, five men worked at putting it into type, and finally the five sections were collected together on a "galley" or long narrow brass pan. A proof was taken and rushed down to Mr. Emberg so that he might see it was all right, but by this time, some typographical errors in the story having been corrected, men were placing it in the "form" or steel frame which holds enough type to make a page of the paper. This was soon in readiness for the stereotyping department.

Larry had not finished the third page of his story before the first two were in type. He hurried through it, and by the time he had handed in the last sheet there were men upstairs waiting for it, so quickly is the mechanical part of newspaper making accomplished.

Finally the story was all in type, the lead lines were in the form, and, when the latter was filled it was "locked," or tightly fastened, and was ready for the men who were to take an impression of the page in damp papier-mache.

This papier-mache, which is also called a matrix, was baked hard by steam, put in a curved cylinder, melted lead was poured on it and there was a solid metal page of the paper ready for the great press, which was soon thundering away, printing thousands of papers, each one containing, on the front page, Larry's account of the interview with Sullivan.

Of course many things had been going on meanwhile. Mr. Emberg had written a "scare head," as they are called, that is a head to be printed in big letters, and this had been set up by men working by hand. This was put on the story after it was in the form.

"Guess Newton is having trouble finding Potter," commented the city editor, when he had finished with Larry's copy. "If we don't hear from him in five minutes we'll miss the edition."

The five minutes passed, and no word came from Harvey Newton. The building shook as the giant press started, and Mr. Emberg, shutting up his watch with a snap, remarked:

"Too late! Well, maybe he'll catch him for the second."

It is often the case that only part of a story gets in the first edition of a paper. So many circumstances govern the getting of news, and the sending of it into the office, that unless a story is obtained, complete, early in the morning it is necessary to make additions to it from edition to edition in the case of an afternoon paper.

"Mack, maybe you'd better try to find Potter," went on Mr. Emberg after a pause, turning to another reporter. "You know him. Tell him we've got an interview with Sullivan, and ask him what the support of Reilly means."

Mack, whose name in full was McConnigan, but who was never designated as anything but "Mack," glanced at the proofs of Larry's story.

"I guess I'll find him in Donnegan's place," he said, naming a resort where men of wealth frequently gathered for lunch. "I'll try there."

"Anywhere to find him," returned the city editor.

"Are you looking for Hamden Potter?" asked an old man, coming into the city room at that juncture.

"That's what we are," said the city editor. "Why, do you know where to find him, Mr. Hogan? Have you got a story for us to-day?"

Hogan was an old newspaper man, never showing any great talents, and he had seen his best days. He was not to be relied on any more, though he frequently took "tips" around to the different papers, receiving for them, together with what money he could beg or borrow, enough to live on.

"I've got a story, yes. I was down at the steamship dock of the Blue Star line a while ago, and I see Mr. Potter's family come off a vessel.

"Was he with them? Have you got the story?" demanded Mr. Emberg, eagerly.

"I've got everything, I guess. I've got all but the main facts, anyhow. I don't know whether Potter was with them or not. I didn't think it was of any importance."

"Importance!" exclaimed the city editor. Then he bethought him of Hogan's character, and knew it was useless to speak. "Everything but the facts—the most important fact of all," Mr. Emberg murmured.

"Isn't that tip worth something?" demanded Hogan.

"Oh, I suppose so," and Mr. Emberg wrote out an order on the cashier for two dollars. Poor Hogan shuffled from the room. He was but a type of many who have outlived their usefulness.

"Jump down to the Blue Star dock, Mack," the city editor said, when Hogan had gone. "Find out all you can about the Potters—where they have been and where Mr. Potter went. Hurry now!"

As Mack was going out the telephone rang. It was a message from Mr. Newton to the effect that he could not find Mr. Potter, and that at his office it was said he was still in Europe.

"Hurry to his house," said Mr. Emberg over the wire. "I have a tip that his family just got in on the *Messina* of the Blue Star line. I've sent Mack to the dock! You go to the house!"

Thus, like a general directing his forces, did the city editor send his men out after news.

CHAPTER X

THREATS AGAINST LARRY

Second edition-time was close at hand, but no news regarding Mr. Hamden Potter had come in from either Newton or Mack. From a reporter sent to interview representatives of the company constructing the subway came a message to the effect that none of the officers would talk for publication.

"What in the world is the matter with Harvey and Mack?" asked Mr. Emberg, restlessly pacing the floor. Every one in the city room felt the strain. Every time the telephone bell rang, the city editor jumped to answer it, without waiting for one of the boys or a reporter to get to the instrument.

Finally, after several false alarms, the bell rang and the city editor, grabbing up the portable telephone, cried out:

"Yes? Oh, it's you, Newton. Where in the world have you been? We only have time for the last edition. Talk fast! What's that? The Potter family home, and you can't see Mr. Potter? Why not? Tell them you've got to see him. Send in a message you have something of importance to tell him. You say you have? And you can't see him? But you must! Go back and try again. This is the biggest story we've had in a long while and we can't fall down on it this way!"

He hung up the receiver on the hook with a bang, and once more began pacing the floor.

"That's queer," he murmured. "There's something strange back of all this. Potter is up to some game, and so is Sullivan. Come here, Larry."

Mr. Emberg closely questioned the young reporter as to every detail of his interview with Sullivan.

"I'm going to write something myself," the city editor announced. "We've got to have more of this story. I can guess at part of it, and I'll make it general enough, and with sufficient 'understoods' in it to save us in case I'm wrong."

He began to write, nervously and hurriedly, handing the sheets over to his assistant to edit as fast as he was done with them. They were rushed upstairs, one at a time, as Larry's copy had been.

The last edition went to press without the much-desired interview with Mr. Potter. The city editor wrote a story, full of glittering generalities, telling how it was believed that certain forces were at work in the interest of getting a new line of the subway through the eighth district, and that Assemblyman Reilly was concerned in the matter, as was also a certain well-known financier, whose name was not mentioned, but whom the readers of the *Leader* would have little difficulty in recognizing as Mr. Potter.

To show that it was Mr. Potter to whom he was referring Mr. Emberg added at the bottom of the story, and under a separate single-line head, a note to the effect that all efforts were unavailing to get an interview with Hamden Potter, the financier, who that day had returned from Europe with his family, as Mr. Potter would see no reporters. It was added that Mr. Potter's connection with the subway interests might throw some light on the reason for the declaration of Sullivan for Reilly.

In all this there was no direct statement made, but the inferences were almost as strong as though the paper had come out boldly and stated as facts what Mr. Emberg believed to be true, but which he dared not assert boldly. But as long as they were not made direct and positive there was no chance for a libel suit, which is something all newspapers dread.

"There, I guess that will do if Harvey can't get at Potter," spoke Mr. Emberg when he had finished. "Queer, though, that Potter keeps himself away from our reporters. He used to be willing enough to talk."

A little later another telephone message was received from Mr. Newton, announcing that it was useless to try to see the millionaire.

"Come on in, then," the city editor directed.

Nor was Mack any more successful. He had learned that the Potter family had hurried from the dock in a closed carriage and were driven to their handsome home on the fashionable thoroughfare known as Central Park, West. No one had seen Mr. Potter, as far as Mack could learn, and the reporter was not allowed to go aboard the ship, as the custom officers were engaged in looking over the baggage of the passengers.

"Well, we've got a good story," said Mr. Emberg late that afternoon, when work for the day was over. "It's a beat, too."

"Did any of 'em make lifts for it?" asked Mr. Hylard, the assistant city editor. A "lift," it may be explained, is the insertion of a piece of news in the last edition of a paper. It is made by taking one plate from the press, removing or "lifting" a comparatively unimportant item of news from the form, inserting the new item, which was received too late for the regular edition, making a new plate, and starting the press again. It is done rather than print an entire new edition, and is sometimes used when some other paper gets a beat or piece of news which your paper must have, or in case of an accident happening after the last edition has gone to press.

"The *Star* lifted our story almost word for word," said Mr. Emberg. "Guess they didn't take the trouble to confirm it. The morning sheets will probably try to discount it."

Which was exactly what they did. Some had what purported to be interviews with Sullivan, denying that he had said he was going to support Reilly. Others showed, editorially and otherwise, how nonsensical it would be for Sullivan to throw his influence to any one but Kilburn.

"I hope you haven't made any mistake, Larry," said Mr. Emberg the next day. "If you misquoted Sullivan it means a bad thing for our paper."

"I quoted him correctly."

At that moment the telephone on Mr. Emberg's desk rang and he answered it.

"Dexter?" he repeated. "Yes, we have a reporter of that name here." Larry was all attention at once. "Who wants him? Oh, Mr. Sullivan? Is this Mr. Sullivan? Well, this is the city editor of the *Leader*. I see some of the papers are denying our story. Our account is about correct, eh? Well, I'm glad of it. Yes, I'll send Mr. Dexter to see you right away."

"Sullivan wants to see you, Larry," went on Mr. Emberg, hanging up the telephone receiver. "This may be a big thing. Go slow and be careful of what he says. Don't let him bluff you."

"You're getting right into politics," said Mr. Newton to Larry, as the young reporter prepared to go out.

"Yes, and I'm afraid I'll get into water where I can't swim."

"Don't let that worry you. You've got to learn, and in New York politics is the most important news of all."

Larry found Sullivan in the same place where he had secured the momentous interview. The Assembly leader nodded to the boy, and then picked up a copy of the paper which contained an account of the talk with Sullivan.

"You made quite a yarn of this," Sullivan remarked.

"Yes, it was a good story."

"A little too good," went on the politician. "You got me into hot water."

"Did I misquote you?"

"No, but you got the information before I was ready to give it out. I thought you knew more than you did. This last part," pointing to the generalities written by Mr. Emberg, "this last part shows that you folks are up a tree. Now I want to know where you heard that about Potter, and I'm going to have an answer," and Sullivan lost his calm air and looked angrily at Larry.

"I can't tell you where I got my tip."

"You mean you will not?"

"Well, you can put it that way," replied Larry.

"I'll make you!" and the politician arose from his chair and stood threateningly over the young reporter. For a moment Larry's heart beat rapidly in fear. Then he remembered what Mr. Emberg had said: "Don't let him bluff you." He was sure Sullivan was bluffing.

"Are you going to tell?" asked Sullivan again.

"I am not."

Sullivan banged his fist down on his desk. He shoved his hat on the back of his head. Thrusting his face close to Larry's he exclaimed:

"Then I'll put you out of business! I'll make the city too hot to hold you! I'll have you fired from the *Leader*, and no other paper in New York will hire you! I'll show you what it is to have Jack Sullivan down on you! I was going to play fair with you. But you sneaked in here and got information I wasn't ready to give out. Now you can take the consequences!"

"I didn't sneak in here!" cried Larry. "I came openly. What's more, you can't scare me! I'm not afraid of you! I know what I did was all right! Perhaps the *Leader* knows more than you think. I'm not going to tell where I got my information, and you can do as you please!"

Sullivan had cooled down. He was a bit ashamed of having given way to his anger, for usually he kept his temper.

"All right," he said. "It's war between us now. Tell your city editor he needn't send you to get any more news from me, and when the *Leader* wants any favors from Jack Sullivan it can whistle for 'em. I'm done with that sheet. I'll show 'em who Sullivan is!"

Larry turned and went out. It was the first time he had been browbeaten like this, but he kept his nerve. If he had only known it, Sullivan was not the first politician to threaten to annihilate a paper, nor was it Sullivan's initial attempt to scare reporters into doing what he wanted.

As Larry left the headquarters he met Peter Manton going in.

"Making up another fake interview with Sullivan?" asked Peter, with a sneer. "You've made a nice mess of it!"

"I didn't make any worse one than you did with that wreck story," retorted Larry, who could not forego this thrust at his old enemy.

"I'll get even with you yet," exclaimed the rival reporter, as he scowled at Larry, and entered Sullivan's private room.

"I wonder what Sullivan will do about it?" thought Larry, as he went back to the office.

CHAPTER XI

A MISSING MILLIONAIRE

Contrary to Larry's expectations Mr. Emberg was not at all impressed by Sullivan's threats.

"I've heard talk like that before," the city editor said. "The *Leader* will try to worry along without the aid of Mr. Jack Sullivan. As for you, Larry, don't give it another thought. If he ever bothers you, or any of his ward-heelers try to make the least trouble for you, let me know. I guess we have some influence in this city. Well, I'll look for wholesale denials of your interview from now on. Sullivan showed his hand too quickly it seems. We must try for Potter now. Queer how he hangs back when we've got part of the story."

"Haven't any of the boys been able to find him?" asked Larry.

"Harvey can't get near him, and when he can't no one can. There's something queer about it. At the house they will give out no information, except to say that Mr. Potter can't be seen. At his office the clerks either say that he is engaged or has not come in yet. I'm beginning to think he's keeping out of the way on purpose."

Mr. Emberg's surmise about the other papers publishing denials of the Sullivan interview was correct. Those journals which were on the same political platform as that of the man whose enmity Larry had incurred proved, to their own satisfaction at least, that Sullivan could not support Reilly. As for the *Leader*, which was independent in politics, that paper did not worry over the accusations of "faking" made against it. Mr. Emberg knew he was right, and he was planning for a big disclosure when some of his reporters could find Hamden Potter.

For a time the Sullivan matter was dropped, and Larry found his time busily occupied in a varied lot of assignments.

One day the young reporter was sent to one of the hotels to interview a youthful millionaire, who had come to the city from a distant town in a big touring car, accompanied by a number of friends.

"Hump! Seems to me I'm assigned to all the millionaire cases," mused Larry.

The young millionaire was named Dick Hamilton, and he was none other than the youth who has figured in another series of mine, called the "Dick Hamilton Series," starting with "Dick Hamilton's Fortune." Dick had come to New York for the purpose of making an investment and had had an encounter with a sharper, who had tried to sell him some worthless stocks.

"Please give me the story," pleaded Larry, and he got the tale in detail, and what was more, he and Dick Hamilton became so friendly that the young millionaire promised to keep the story from all other reporters; so that Larry scored another beat, much to his own satisfaction and the satisfaction of his friends.

"Keep on and you'll be at the top," said the city editor, and then he went on: "Here is something else you might look into, Larry. It might make a fine thing for the Sunday supplement. You can go up there, get the yarn, and you needn't come back to-day. Write it up the first thing in the morning."

"What sort of story is it?" asked Larry.

"Why, it's a postal, from an old German, I take it, who says he has invented a flying machine."

"I guess he's about the only one in ten thousand who has been successful then," answered Larry, smiling.

"Oh, I don't suppose it amounts to anything," went on Mr. Emberg. "But it may make a good story to let the old gentleman talk, and describe the machine. The public likes stories about flying machines and queer inventors, even if the machines don't work. Get a good yarn, for we need one for the first page of the supplement. I'll sent Sneed, the photographer, up later to get some pictures of it."

The city editor handed Larry a postal card, poorly written and spelled, on which there was a request that a reporter be sent to a certain address on the East Side, to get a story of a wonderful invention, destined to revolutionize methods of travel.

It was not the first time Larry had been sent on this sort of an assignment. Once he had gone to get a story of a new kind of gas lamp a man had invented, and the thing had exploded while he was watching the owner demonstrate it. Luckily neither of them were hurt.

Larry found the address given on the postal was in a dilapidated tenement, seemingly deserted, and standing some distance away from other buildings.

When he got there he ran into a reporter named Fritsch, who worked on a German newspaper.

"Dot inventor vos mofed avay," said the German reporter. "Some beoples told me he vos krazy."

"Is the house vacant?" asked Larry.

"I dink so. Maype ve walk through him, yah?"

Larry was willing, and together the pair went into the tenement and upstairs.

As they passed through one of the halls Larry looked up and saw a man peering down at him over a balustrade. He gave a gasp.

"Vot it is?" questioned the German reporter.

"That man!" cried Larry. He ran up the stairs and tried to catch the individual, who was running away.

The man was the person he had helped to rescue from the ocean—the one who had given his name as Mah Retto.

The strange man entered a side room and locked the door. Larry knocked, but nobody answered his summons.

"Dot vos not der inventor," said Fritsch.

"I know it—but I'd like to see him, nevertheless," answered the young newspaper man.

A little later the two reporters came down into the street and separated. Larry went home, but after supper that evening he walked again in the direction of the lonely tenement. He wanted to see the policeman, whose post took in that section of the city, and make some inquiries of him. The officer might be able to throw some light on the sudden appearance of the strange man.

Larry found the policeman after some search. The officer, as soon as he learned Larry was from the *Leader*, was very willing to tell all he knew, for the *Leader* was a paper that always spoke well of the police, and the force appreciated this.

"It sure is a queer house," said Patrolman Higgins. "I remember the time it was filled with families, but they all moved away because the owner didn't make any repairs. The only person there was a crazy German who's daffy on airships. He got out to-day."

"I've heard of him," replied Larry. "But is he the only one in there? I heard there was another man stopping there."

"Now that you speak of it, I shouldn't wonder but what there was," answered Higgins. "I saw two lights in there to-night, for the first time. I've got sort of used to seeing one in the window where the crazy German is puttering away at his airship, but awhile ago I noticed a gleam in another part of the house. I took it for a second lamp the German had lighted, but now that I think of it, seems to me it was on the other side of the house. I shouldn't wonder but what you're right."

"Oh, it doesn't matter much," said Larry, who did not want to arouse too great interest in the matter. "I just thought you might happen to know him."

"I'll make some inquiries in the neighborhood," the officer went on. "I don't want that shack to get to be a hanging-out place for tramps. It was bad enough to have the German there, but he paid his rent to the owner, who's about as crazy as the airship inventor. I'll look up this other fellow. Drop around to-morrow night and I may have some news for you."

"I will," replied Larry, satisfied that he had put his plan into operation. "It's nothing special, but I had an idea I might get a story out of the chap." And he went home again.

Larry reported to Mr. Emberg the next morning all the details of the visit to the strange house.

"If some East Indian chooses to hide himself it can't make much difference to us," said the city editor. "I judge him to be a native from that name. I've got another story for you to go out on. It's about——"

At that instant the telephone on Mr. Emberg's desk rang insistently. He broke off what he was saying to Larry to grab up the instrument.

"Hello. Yes, this is Mr. Emberg. Oh, is that you, Harvey? What's that? Reported to the police as missing? Are you sure it's him? Great Scott! If that's true that's a corking good story! That explains some things! You take the police end and I'll send some one up to the house! Good-bye!"

The city editor was excited.

"Here, Larry!" he cried. "Jump right out on this. The police have just received a report that Hamden Potter, the millionaire financier, is missing. They tried to keep it quiet, but Harvey got on to it. Hustle up to Potter's house and get all the particulars you can. Get a picture of him. Hamden Potter missing!" he went on, as Larry hurried away on his assignment. "There's something queer in the wind, that's sure!"

There was—something more strange than Mr. Emberg suspected, and Larry's assignment was one destined to last for some time.

CHAPTER XII

A BRAVE GIRL

Hamden Potter lived in one of the finest houses in New York. Larry had often admired it as he walked in the neighborhood of Central Park, in which vicinity many other New York millionaires have their residences.

"Now I've got a chance to see the inside," thought Larry, as he sat in the elevated train, and was whirled along toward his destination. "That is if they let me in. Guess I'll have my hands full getting information up there. Still, if I work it right, I may learn all I want to know."

There are only two general classes of persons from whom reporters can get news. One class is that which is only too ready to impart it, for their own ends and interests, and this news is seldom the kind the papers want. The other class consists of persons who are determined that they will give no information to the representatives of the press. This class usually has the very news that the papers want, and the journals strive all the more eagerly to get it, from the very fact that there is a desire to hold it from them. Both classes must be approached in ways best suited to them; the one that they may not take up a reporter's valuable time with a lot of useless talk, and the other that they may be tricked into giving out that which they are determined to keep back. It was to the latter class that Larry was going that morning. On his way up he was turning over in his mind the best means of getting what he wanted.

"Some butler or private secretary will come to the door," he reasoned. "I've got to get in to see a member of the family. There's only Mrs. Potter and her daughter Grace," for, in common with other rich men and those in the public eye, Mr. Potter's family affairs were, in a measure, public property to the New York newspaper world.

As Larry had surmised, his ring at the door was answered by a stately butler.

"I wish to see Mr. Potter," said the reporter, venturing on a bold stroke. He had learned several tricks of the trade.

"Mr. Potter is not home," and the door was about to close.

"Will you take a message to Mrs. Potter?" asked Larry quickly.

The door was opened a little.

"What name?" and the butler did not relax his severity.

"It doesn't matter what name. Tell her I have called in reference to Mr. Potter's absence."

"Come in!" the butler exclaimed quickly.

Larry had gained his first skirmish, in a manner perfectly legitimate, regarded from a newspaper standpoint. He had called in reference to Mr. Potter's disappearance—not to give information (as the butler may have supposed), but to get it.

"This way," said the man. "Mrs. Potter is in the library."

Larry entered through the velvet portieres the butler held aside for him. He saw, reclining on a couch, a handsome woman, whose face showed traces of tears. Beside her stood the most beautiful girl Larry had ever seen. She had brown eyes, brown hair, and a face that, though it was sad, made Larry think of some wonderful painting.

"Some one with news of Mr. Potter," the butler announced.

"Oh! Have you come to tell me of my husband?" the lady exclaimed, sitting up suddenly.

Larry's mind was working quickly. If he took the right means he was liable to get the information he wanted. On the other hand he was in a fair way to be shown the door indignantly, for he realized that he had entered under false pretenses, however honorable his motives might have been.

"I beg your pardon for intruding," he said, speaking quickly. "I have come to ask news of Mr. Potter, not to bring it. One moment," as he saw Mrs. Potter's face assume a look of anger. "His disappearance has been reported to the police. They tried to keep it quiet, but it was impossible in the case of a man of Mr. Potter's standing. Our paper—the *Leader*—knows of it. In a short time it will be known to every paper in New York. I think it would be wise for you to meet the situation, and give me whatever information you can. We will only be too glad to help you locate your husband, and I believe there is no better way than by newspaper publicity, even the police will tell you that. If you could give me a description of the missing man, when he was last seen, what sort of clothing he wore, and a picture of him we will publish it in the paper.

Thousands of persons will see the account and will be on the lookout for him. Believe me, it is the best way!"

Larry paused for breath. He had rattled all that off without giving Mrs. Potter a chance to stop him, for he wanted to present his case in the most advantageous light.

"Mamma, I believe he is right!" exclaimed Grace Potter. "I never thought of it that way before. I thought the newspaper people were horrid when any one had trouble."

"We are human," said Larry with a little laugh, and Grace smiled, though her eyes had traces of tears.

"I could not think of discussing your father's affairs with a reporter," said Mrs. Potter stiffly.

"I don't want to pry into his affairs," returned Larry. "I only want to help you find him."

"But this publicity is so disgraceful!"

"Not at all, madam. It is a misfortune, perhaps, but other families have the same trouble. Nothing is thought of it. The newspapers are the best means of tracing lost persons."

"That's right, mother," interrupted Grace. "I often read descriptions of persons who have disappeared, and a few days later I see that they have been found, principally through an account in the paper. I am sure this young gentleman will help us."

"I will do all I can," said Larry. "So will the other papers, I am sure. Now when did he disappear? Is this a picture of him?" and he took one from the library table. "Suppose you let me take this to have a cut made of it. I will return it," and before Mrs. Potter or Grace could object Larry had it in his pocket. That is the way reporters get along sometimes, by taking advantage of every opportunity. Once lost these golden chances seldom can be seized again.

Before mother or daughter could answer Larry's question the door bell rang, and, a moment later, the butler announced:

"Some newspaper reporters, madam!"

"Oh, this is dreadful! I can't see them!" exclaimed Mrs. Potter. "Tell them to go away. Let them see Mr. Potter's lawyer!"

"Mother, let me attend to this for you," said Grace. "I will see the reporters. I will tell them all that is necessary. I'm not afraid. I want to find poor, dear papa!"

"You are a brave girl," murmured Mrs. Potter, as she wiped her eyes. "I would not dare face them all in our trouble."

Larry agreed with Mrs. Potter's characterization of Grace. It was no easy task for a girl of eighteen to thus assume the responsibility, but she had the courage, and Larry admired her for it.

"You had better go to your room, mother," Grace went on. "I will see the newspaper men in here," she added to the butler who was waiting. "You may stay," she said, looking at Larry, "and you will learn all we ourselves know."

Larry realized there was no opportunity for a beat in this matter of the disappearance of the millionaire, as the news the police get they give out indiscriminately to all papers. So he was content to get what information he needed in common with the other reporters. But he had a picture, and he doubted if all the others would get one.

The butler showed the reporters in. They were nearly all young men, about Larry's age, though one or two were gray-haired veterans of the pencil.

"What is it you wish to inquire about first?" asked Grace, as she faced the newspaper men, more calmly than could her mother, who had gone to her room.

CHAPTER XIII

WHERE IS HE?

"When did Mr. Potter run away?" asked a voice from the group of press representatives, and Larry saw it was his old enemy, Peter Manton, of the *Scorcher*—a sensational sheet—who had made the inquiry.

"My father didn't run away!" exclaimed Grace indignantly. "If you are going on that assumption I shall give you no information at all."

"That was a mistake," interposed an elderly reporter. "We are only anxious to know when you last saw him," and someone whispered a well-deserved rebuke to Peter.

"To begin at the beginning," Grace resumed, "father went abroad with mother and me several months ago. He was not in good health and his physician recommended a change of air. We traveled in England and on the continent, and then went to Italy. My father preceded us there, as he had some business affairs to look after in Rome.

"When we got to that city we found he had left there, as his business called him away. He left word that he might have to sail for this country ahead of us, but would try to meet us in Naples. We proceeded there, only to find that he had sailed, and he told us to come over on the next steamer. He promised to meet us in New York.

"We sailed on the *Messina*, expecting my father would meet us at the pier."

"Did he meet you?" asked Larry, for he recalled that day when he had secured the memorable interview with Sullivan, in which Mr. Potter's name played an important part.

"He did not," and there was a catch in the girl's voice. "One of his clerks did, and said he had received a letter from my father, stating that he was unavoidably detained, but that he would be with us soon."

She paused, and pressed her handkerchief to her eyes.

"Well?" asked one of the reporters softly.

"That is all," said Grace. "I have not seen my father since parting with him at Munich, whence he proceeded to Rome. He has never communicated directly with us, and we don't know what to think. It is dreadful!" and she wept softly.

There was a pause of a few seconds, while the girl recovered her composure. Then the reporters began to ask questions, sparing Grace as much as possible.

In this way they learned that Mr. Potter's family could give no description as to was dressed when he disappeared, for quite an interval had elapsed between the time Grace and her mother had last seen him, and when they learned that he was gone.

Nor had Mr. Potter communicated with his office or his business associates, except so far as to send a clerk to meet the steamer. Before going to Europe he had arranged matters so his affairs could be conducted in his absence, and his continued failure to come back worked no harm in that respect. Confidential clerks attended to everything, and the millionaire's large interests were well looked after.

So there was really not much that Grace could tell. She said she and her mother had waited some time, after getting home, hoping Mr. Potter would come back or communicate with them, but when he had not done so they became alarmed. They feared he had met with some mishap, and, after talking the matter over with his lawyers, they had decided it would be best to report the matter to the police.

"We are much obliged to you," said Larry, when it seemed that no more questions were necessary.

"We'll do our best, through the papers, to help find your father," added a gray-haired reporter.

"Now give us his picture," put in Peter Manton, in a commanding tone.

"We have none to give out at present," said Grace coldly. "We are having a number made, showing him as he looked when he went away, and they will be ready in a few days. The lawyers will attend to that, if my father is not found in the meanwhile."

"We've got to have a picture now!" exclaimed Peter.

"You shut up!"—thus in a whisper, from another reporter who stood near the representative of the *Scorcher*. "You don't know when you've been treated decent. Half the millionaire families in New York wouldn't even let us inside the door, let alone telling us all we wanted to know. Dry up!" And Peter desisted after that rebuke.

Larry managed to be the last one of the reporters to leave the house. He lingered in the hall, and when he and Grace were there alone he said:

"One thing I forgot to ask. When you got back to the house was there any evidence that your father had been here ahead of you? Was the house shut up while you were in Europe?"

"I'm glad you spoke of that," the girl replied. "I had forgotten about it. Yes, the house was closed all the while we were away, and opened the day mother and I got back. But, now that you speak of it, I recollect something that seemed strange at the time. We were a little worried when father did not meet us at the pier, and I had an idea that he might have spent some nights in the house, pending our arrival, though he had said in his letters that if he came over ahead of us he was going to stop at a hotel. I went to his room——"

She broke into tears again, and Larry waited, looking out of the big front doors, for he was embarrassed.

"When I looked over his room," continued Grace, going on bravely, "I saw something was missing, that I knew was on his dresser when we left for Europe."

"What was it?" asked Larry.

"It was a little picture of mother and myself. My father was very fond of it. He must have come to the house and taken it—one of his last acts before he disappeared. It made me feel very sad when I thought of it afterward."

"Perhaps he took the picture to Europe with him, and you did not know it," suggested Larry, who was beginning to develop the instincts of a detective, as all reporters do, more or less.

"No," said Grace positively. "I remember, I was the last one in father's room before we sailed for Europe. The carriage was waiting to take us to the pier, and father went out just ahead of me. He spoke of the picture then, saying he would leave it to keep guard over his room until he came back," and once more Grace could not keep back her tears.

"Could the picture have been stolen?" asked Larry.

"The house was in perfect order when we came in," said the girl. "Nothing else was missing. It seems as if father took that picture to—to remind him of us—and—and that we would never see him again."

"Oh, yes, you will!" exclaimed Larry heartily. "You will find him all right. Perhaps he has some business matters to attend to out West, and hasn't time to come home."

"He could have written."

"Maybe he is some place where the mails are infrequent."

Thus Larry tried to comfort Grace, but it was hard work, for the disappearance of Hamden Potter certainly was strange and difficult to explain.

"I will let you know if we hear any news," said Larry as he prepared to go.

"Will you? That will be very kind of you. I thank you very much for your help. I would never have known what to do if it had not been for your suggestions. Come any time you have any news for us—and I hope you will come soon—and often," Grace added with a blush.

Larry's heart beat a little faster than usual, for it was not every day he received such an invitation to a millionaire's house, nor from such a pretty girl as Grace.

"Afraid I'll not have much chance, though," he thought to himself as he went down the steps. "I'll probably be taken off this case after to-day, and some other reporter will get it. If I had a little more experience they might let me work on it. Never mind, I'll get there some day," and with this Larry comforted himself.

___

CHAPTER XIV

IN THE TENEMENT HOUSE

The story of Hamden Potter's disappearance, as Larry wrote it, made interesting reading. He used that part about the picture which Grace had told him, but which the other reporters did not know about. The photograph of the missing millionaire, which showed a man in the prime of life, with a large moustache, came out well in the paper, and as Larry saw the article, on the front page, under a "big head," he could not but feel he had done well.

In this he was confirmed by the city editor, who, seeing copies of the other afternoon papers, as they were brought in to him, exclaimed:

"Well, Larry, you did fine!"

"How's that?" asked the youth.

"Why you've got 'em all beat on the picture proposition, and none of 'em have that part about his coming back to the house and taking the miniature of his wife and daughter. That's the best part of the whole yarn."

"I got that by luck, almost at the last minute, when the others were gone," said Larry.

"That's the kind of luck that makes big stories," commented Mr. Emberg. "You might take a run up to the house this evening and see if there's anything new, and then you can pay a visit in the morning. I'll have the police end looked after by Harvey, and I'll send a man to Mr. Potter's office. It's barely possible he may turn up there any minute. I have an idea that he is temporarily insane because of his heavy business responsibilities, and that he has wandered off somewhere. He'll come back in a few days. What do you think about it yourself, Larry?"

"I hardly know what to think. I never was on a case like this before. When I first heard about his taking the picture away I thought maybe he had gone off somewhere to commit suicide, and wanted it with him."

"No suicide for Hamden Potter," put in Harvey Newton, with a laugh, as he stood listening to Larry and Mr. Emberg talking. "He has too much to live for."

"Well, I didn't want to think that," Larry went on. "He has a very fine wife and——"

"And a beautiful daughter," broke in Harvey. "Look out, Larry, this is not a love story you're working on."

Larry blushed like a girl, for several times that day he had caught himself thinking of Grace and how pretty she was.

"Let Larry alone for getting all the facts in the case," said Mr. Emberg. "I suppose Miss Grace gave you some information?"

"She talked to all the reporters," Larry said. "Mrs. Potter is a nervous wreck."

"Well, run up any time this evening," went on the city editor. "You might stumble on some news. You wrote a very good story to-day. Try again to-morrow. We've beat the other papers on it as it is."

Larry got Mr. Potter's picture back from the art department, where a cut for use in the paper had been made, and decided that he would have a good excuse for calling at the Potter residence in going back to return it as he had promised.

"I wish I had some news to tell her," the young reporter thought as he went home to supper, "but it's too soon yet. I'd like to be a detective and see if I couldn't find her father for her. I wonder where he can be, or why he disappeared? Of course, if he's out of his mind, as Mr. Emberg believes, that would account for it, but I don't think he is."

Telling his mother he did not expect to be out long, Larry left the house early that evening. He intended to go to Mr. Potter's residence, leave the picture, have a few minutes' talk with Grace, and then go home by way of the street on which the tenement was located, where he had undergone the queer experience with the crazy inventor.

"Maybe the policeman has discovered something new about that strange man from the wreck," thought Larry.

He found Grace more composed than when he had seen her in the afternoon.

"Did you bring me any news?" she asked, as she took the picture.

"I'm sorry, but I couldn't. I will, though, if there is any to bring. I'm sure your father will be found."

"So am I!" exclaimed the girl. "Poor mother is in despair, but I am not going to give up. If the police can't find him I'm going to make a search myself. I know a great deal about his business. Father always said I ought to have been a boy."

Larry thought it would have been a pity, but he did not say so.

"I'll search all over until I find him," Grace went on.

"And I'll help you!" cried Larry, fired to sudden enthusiasm.

"Will you? Really? That will be fine!" and, before she was aware of what she was doing, Grace had held out her hand. Larry gave it a firm grip, and the girl blushed.

"I suppose I shouldn't have done that!" she said. "I'm always doing things on impulse. I don't even know your name. I must call you Mr. Reporter," and she smiled.

"I'm Larry Dexter," said our hero, blushing a bit himself. "I know your name, so now I suppose we may consider ourselves introduced."

"I guess so, though it isn't strictly according to form. But never mind. This is no time for ceremonies. I hope you will have news for me—soon."

"So do I," answered Larry as he took his leave.

The young reporter was soon in that neighborhood of the city where was situated the deserted tenement in which he believed there was some mystery. As he approached the ramshackle old structure he noticed a figure pacing up and down in front of it.

"If that's the lunatic inventor of the airship I think I'll pass on the other side," Larry said to himself. It was dark in that section of the city, the electric lights being few and far between. However, as the figure approached, and as Larry continued on, the youth saw he had nothing to fear, for it was that of his friend, Policeman Higgins.

"Well," asked Larry, as he came up. "Anything new?"

This is the reporter's form of greeting to almost everyone he meets, and means: "Have you any news for me?"

"Good-evening," replied Officer Higgins. "I was just thinking about you."

"Nothing bad, I hope."

"No, I was wishing you'd happen along. You remember we were talking the other night about a strange man that you thought was in here?"

"Yes."

"Well, he's in here now, and I'm going to see what he's up to. The crazy old professor, with his airship, has moved out, and the house is deserted except for this new bird. I'm going to raid his nest, for I suspect he's up to no good. I've been watching his light for some time, and he's moving around in several rooms. Maybe he's going to set fire to the place."

"Going to tackle him alone?" asked Larry.

"No, I've telephoned to the sergeant to send me a man to help me go through the shack, for though I'm not a coward I've no hankering to go in that shell after dark, knowing a man may be waiting for me with a knife or a gun."

"I'll stay here and see what happens," said Larry.

"Come along in with us if you like," went on Higgins, for he had taken a liking to the young reporter. "You may get a story out of it. Here comes Storg now," he added, as the form of another bluecoat was seen approaching down the street.

The two officers held a brief consultation. Higgins showed where a light was nickering back and forth between two rooms on one side of the building, about the third story up.

"It's been going that way for the last hour," said Higgins. "I'm going in now. Get your gun ready, Storg. You may not need it, but, if you do, it's best to have it handy."

Larry followed behind the policemen, his heart beating a little faster than usual. He was anxious to see the man who was in hiding, and who, he believed, was the same one he and the fisherman had rescued from the sea. He believed there was a mystery connected with the fugitive which would make a good story, even if he was an East Indian.

"Easy now," cautioned Higgins, but Larry thought it was needless, as the heavy shoes of the officers made noise enough to awaken the soundest sleeper.

The bluecoats entered the dark hallway of the tenement. The doors were void of locks and swung to and fro, creaking on rusty hinges, as the wind blew them. There was a damp and unpleasant smell in the house, and now and then came queer sounds, that echoed through the deserted rooms.

"Nothing but shutters banging," explained Higgins, as his companion-in-arms started. "They're flapping like a bird's broken wing, all over the place. Now for our mysterious friend."

But for the fact that both officers carried small pocket electric lamps, operated by dry batteries, they would have had difficulty in making their way through the halls and up the stairs, for there were many holes, caused by rotting boards. As it was they moved along with some speed, until they came to the third floor.

"He'll be about here somewhere," whispered Higgins, a needless precaution, as their advance had been already heralded by their heavy foot-falls.

"There's a light there," said Storg, pointing to the end of a long hall. Coming from under a door could be seen a faint gleam.

"That's where he is!" exclaimed Higgins. "Come on!"

Larry followed the officers. Their steps echoed through the silent building. Forward they went until they came to the door beneath which the light showed. Higgins tried the knob. The portal was locked.

"Let us in! We're police officers!" he exclaimed.

There was a rustling within the room, but no attempt was made to open the door.

"Open or we'll break it in!" cried Higgins, and, as there was no answer, but only silence, he put his big shoulder to the frail door. There was a crackling sound, a splintering of wood and the hinges gave way. Higgins fairly jumped into the room as the portal fell in. Storg followed after him, with his hand on his revolver, ready to use it should occasion arise. But there was no need, for the room was deserted, though a candle burning on a mantel showed there had recently been an occupant in it.

"He's gone!" cried Higgins, looking around.

At that moment there was a sound in the corridor, and somewhere along its length a door opened.

"He's getting away!" yelled Storg, as he jumped back into the hallway. Larry followed, and the policeman flashed his electric lamp.

Then, in the little circle of light cast from the glass bullseye, Larry saw, running down the stairs, the smooth-shaven man he had helped pull from the angry sea on the life-raft.

"There he goes! Catch him!" cried Storg, as he clattered down the stairs after the fugitive.

CHAPTER XV

LARRY'S SPECIAL ASSIGNMENT

"Hold on! Stop!" yelled Higgins, running from the room. "Halt, or I'll shoot!"

It would have done little good had he done so, for by this time the mysterious man was in the second hallway, and out of reach of any possible bullets.

"You stay here and look after things, I'll catch him!" called Storg, as he raced down the stairs, his light making erratic circles as he advanced.

"I guess that's good advice," commented Higgins to Larry, who had remained in the upper corridor. "I'm too fat to run. Let's see what he left behind."

Back into the room, where the candle was burning, went Larry and the policeman. A quick survey showed nothing unusual. There were some old chairs and a table, left probably by the departed tenants.

"He must have had the run of several rooms," Higgins went on. "He came out of some apartment farther down the hall, and that's how he fooled us. He was on the watch, and that shows there must be something queer about him."

"Let's take a look through the other rooms," suggested Larry.

Showing his light Higgins led the way. They went through several other bare and deserted chambers, but saw no indications that the stranger had been in them. Presently they came to what had been a bathroom, though most of the plumbing had been torn out by thieves, for the value of the lead pipes and the faucets.

"He's been here!" cried Larry, as he pointed to a faint spark in one corner of the room.

The policeman flashed his electric on it. It proved to be a candle that had burned down into the socket, the remainder of a wick smouldering and glowing.

"Yes, and he shaved himself here," the officer added, as he pointed to a razor, some soap, and pieces of paper on which were unmistakable evidences that the mysterious man had been acting as his own barber. "I'd like to catch him," the bluecoat went on. "I'm sure there's something crooked about him."

"It looks so," agreed Larry. "Maybe Storg will get him."

"I hope so," and Higgins began to make a more thorough search of the apartment.

There was nothing, however, which shed any further light on the mysterious man. It was evident, though, that he had lived in the deserted house for several days, since there were remnants of food scattered here and there.

"The mystery is getting deeper and deeper," thought Larry. He said nothing to the policeman about the man being a person who had come ashore from the *Olivia*. "I'm going to ask Mr. Emberg to let me work on this case," he resolved, while he followed Higgins from room to room. "I believe it will be a great story if I can get all the details."

How much of a story it was destined to be Larry had no idea of at that moment, though his newspaper instinct, that led him to suspect there was a strange mystery connected with Mah Retto, was perfectly correct, as he learned later.

"Well, I don't see that we can learn anything more here," remarked Higgins when he had been in a number of chambers on the third floor. "He evidently only used a few of these handsome apartments," and he laughed as he looked around on the dilapidated rooms, with the plaster peeling from the walls, the windows half broken, and the doors falling from their hinges.

"Hark!" exclaimed Larry. "Some one is coming!"

Footsteps sounded in the lower hall.

"That's Storg, coming back!" cried Higgins. "I hope he got his man."

He leaned over the balustrade and called down:

"Any luck, Storg?"

"No, he got away," was the reply. "He's a good runner. I couldn't keep up to him."

"Never mind," consoled Higgins. "Maybe it's just as well. We'd have trouble proving anything illegal against him, though I could have had him held on a charge of vagrancy until I investigated a bit."

The officers, followed by Larry, left the ramshackle structure, with the wind whistling mournfully through the broken windows, and the shutters banging, while the doors creaked on the rusty and broken hinges.

"I wouldn't want to stay there all alone at night," thought the young reporter, as he started toward home. "A man must have a strong motive to cause him to hide in there. I'd like to find out what it is. Perhaps I shall, some time."

Larry spoke of the matter to Mr. Emberg the next day. He said he thought it might be a good idea to devote some hours to working up the story, in an endeavor to learn who the queer man was.

"Still puzzling over your East Indian, eh?" asked the city editor. "Well, there may be something in it, but just now I have something else for you to do."

"Another flying-machine story?"

"Not exactly. I'm going to give you a special assignment."

Larry was all attention at once. The best part of the newspaper life is being given a special assignment—that is, put to work on a certain case, to the exclusion of everything else. Every reporter dreams of the time when he shall become a special correspondent or given a special assignment. It means that your time is your own, to a great extent; that you may go and come as you please; that your expense bills are seldom questioned, and that you may travel afar and see strange sights. The only requirement, and it is not an easy one, is that you get the news, and get it in time for the paper. Of course, it need not be said that you must let no other paper beat you, but this seldom occurs, as when a reporter is on a special assignment he works alone, and what he gets is his. There are no other newspaper men to worry him.

So, when Mr. Emberg told Larry there was a special assignment for him, the young reporter's heart beat high with hope. He had often wished for one, but they had never come his way before, though to many on the *Leader* they were an old story.

"What is it?" asked Larry, wondering how far out of town it would take him.

"I want you to find Mr. Potter, the missing millionaire, Larry," said Mr. Emberg.

"Find Mr. Potter?"

"That's it. I want you to devote your whole time to that case. Never mind about anything else. Find Mr. Potter. There's a big story back of his going away; a bigger story than you have any idea of. I don't know what it is myself, but I want you to find out. Now I am going to give you free rein and full swing. Do whatever you think is necessary. Get us news. We'll have to have a story every day, for we're going to play this thing up and feature it. You're going to be on the firing-line, so to speak. Take care of yourself, but don't go to sleep. Get ahead of the other fellows and get us news. That's what we want. That's what makes the *Leader* a success. It's because we get the news, and generally get it first.

"I can't tell you where to start, or what to do. You'll have to find that out for yourself. Get all the information you can from the family. See some of Mr. Potter's business associates. Have another interview with Sullivan. Maybe he knows something about it, though I doubt it.

"At any rate, whatever you do, find Mr. Potter," and at this closing instruction Mr. Emberg learned back in his chair and looked sharply at Larry.

"Suppose I can't," and the young reporter smiled.

"'Can't' isn't in the reporter's dictionary," the city editor replied. "You've got to find him. I don't want to see you fall down. You've done well, so far, Larry. Now's a chance to distinguish yourself."

Larry knew that it was. He also realized that he was going to have his hardest work since he had become a reporter. It was a special assignment, such as any newspaper man might wish for, but it was not one that could be characterized as easy.

"I've got my work cut out for me," thought the youth, as he turned away.

"Here's an order for fifty dollars," went on Mr. Emberg, as he handed the young reporter a slip of paper. "Take it to the cashier, and when you want more for expenses let me know. Don't be afraid of using it if you see a chance to get news, but, of course, don't waste it. Now go, and find Mr. Potter, but don't forget we must have some sort of a story every day."

Larry's first act, after receiving his special assignment, was to go to Mr. Potter's house. Grace received him, and, in answer to his inquiry, stated that the family had no more news than they had at first.

"I thought you could tell us something," said the girl in disappointed tones.

"Perhaps I can, soon," replied Larry. "I'm detailed specially on this case now," and he told her of his assignment.

"Does that mean you have nothing to do but to search for my father?"

"That's what it means."

"Oh, please find him for me!" exclaimed the girl. "You don't know how much I have suffered since he has been missing, nor how much my mother has suffered. It has been terrible! Oh, if you only could find him for us!"

"Miss Potter," began Larry, who was deeply touched by her distress, "a newspaper man could have no greater incentive to work than the duty to which his assignment calls him. More especially in this case to which my city editor has told me to devote my whole time. But aside from that I'm going to find your father for your sake and your mother's. I'll do all I can. I'll work on this case day and night. I'll find your father for you!"

"Oh!" exclaimed Grace, "you don't know how much good it does me to hear you talk so! It seemed as if no one cared. Of course my father's business associates want him to come back, and so do his friends, but—but they don't wish it as much as my mother does and as I do! I miss him so much!"

If Larry had not had the injunction laid on him by Mr. Emberg to urge him on in the search, the appeal by Grace would have been more than sufficient. Hereafter, he resolved, he would feel somewhat as did the knights of old when they were commissioned by their ladies to execute some bold deed.

"Don't worry," he told Grace, as he saw her distress was getting the better of her. "I'll find him."

"Suppose you can't?"

"There's no such work as 'can't' in my dictionary," replied Larry, repeating what Mr. Emberg had told him.

Grace smiled at the young reporter's enthusiasm, but she knew she could have had no better friend, no one who would devote more time and energy to her cause, and no one who had so strong a motive for finding the missing millionaire as had this young newspaper reporter.

While the two were discussing various details of the case there was a ring at the front door, and, presently, the butler entered the library.

"Mr. Jack Sullivan to see you, miss," he announced.

CHAPTER XVI

SULLIVAN'S QUEER ACCUSATION

"Whom did you say it was?" asked Grace.

"Mr. Jack Sullivan," repeated the butler. "I asked him for his card, miss, but he said he hadn't got none. Told me to mention his name, an' said you'd know him."

"But I don't know him," protested Grace. "I never heard of him in my life. There must be some mistake. Are you sure he wants, me, Peterson?"

"He said so, miss, but I'll ask again."

Whereupon the butler, as stiff as a ramrod, went back to the door where he had left Mr. Sullivan standing.

"He means you, miss," the functionary remarked, as he came back to the library.

"I wonder what he can want," Grace said, half to herself. "I don't know any such person. I think there's a mistake. I will see him, and tell him so."

"Wait a minute," exclaimed Larry. "Perhaps I can explain this. I think I know Mr. Sullivan."

"Who is he?"

"A political leader of the eighth assembly district."

"What does that mean; I'm dreadfully ignorant of politics," Grace remarked with a smile. "Poor papa was much interested in them, but I never could make head or tail out of political matters."

"I have an idea that Sullivan has called here in reference to the disappearance of your father."

"Why do you think that?" and Grace turned pale. "Do you think he brings bad news?"

"On the contrary, I think he has come in search of information."

"But how can he be interested?"

Thereupon Larry told of his interview with the politician, based on what he had overheard in reference to Mr. Potter and the extension of the subway.

"Wasn't your father interested in building a new line of street railroad?" he asked of Grace.

"I'm sure I don't know. I never kept track of papa's business matters."

"I see."

"What ought I to do about this Mr. Sullivan?" Grace asked.

"I think you had better see him," replied Larry.

"I'd be afraid to, alone, and mother has such a headache that she can't come downstairs. Will you stay in the room with me?" and she looked appealingly at Larry.

"I'm afraid if I did Sullivan wouldn't talk. He knows me, and imagines I have done him a wrong, which I have not. I believe he considers me his enemy. He would probably go away without saying anything if you met him in my presence."

"But you don't need to be actually present," said Grace, with sudden inspiration. "Look here, this is a little alcove," and she pulled aside a hanging curtain and showed a recess in the library wall. "You can stand in there, and hear whatever he has to say. I'd feel safer if you were near. Of course there's Peterson, but he's so queer, and I don't like the servants to hear too much about poor father's disappearance. Will you stay here and be at hand in case I want you?"

"Of course I will," replied Larry after a moment's hesitation. "I have no idea that Sullivan will annoy you. He's too much of a politician for that. And I may be able to get a clue from what he says, though I don't imagine he knows where Mr. Potter is."

"Then I'll see him," decided Grace. "Peterson," she called.

"Yes, miss."

"You may show Mr. Sullivan in here."

"In here, miss?" and the butler looked at Larry.

"I said in here."

"Very well, miss."

"Now hide," commanded the girl in a whisper, as soon as Peterson had gone to the front door, where Mr. Sullivan had been kept waiting, as the butler evidently thought the caller did not look like a person to be admitted to the hallway until he had showed his credentials, or until he had been authorized to come in by some member of the family.

Larry got behind the curtain. No sooner had the folds ceased shaking than Mr. Sullivan entered the library. Larry could see him, though the young reporter himself was hidden from view. Grace remained standing.

"You wished to see me?" she asked in formal tones.

"Yes, Miss Potter," and Larry noted that Sullivan was ill at ease. "I called about your father."

"Do you know where he is?"

"No, Miss Potter. How should I?" and Sullivan looked quite surprised.

"Then why did you come?"

"I came for some information, miss."

"We have none to give you. We have told the police and the reporters all we know."

"Are you sure?" and at this question Sullivan's bearing became different. He seemed bolder.

"What do you mean?" demanded Grace.

"I mean just this," went on the politician. "I've got a right to know where Mr. Potter is. A great deal depends on it. I've got to find him. Reilly wants to find him. He and Reilly had some deal on, and it's time it was put through. It's going to make trouble if it isn't. I want to know where Mr. Potter is?"

"So do we," answered Grace. "If this is all that you came for you had better leave."

"It isn't all I came for!" Sullivan's voice had an angry ring. "I don't believe you have told the police or the newspapers all you know about this thing. I believe——"

"Leave this room!" commanded Grace. "Leave it at once, or I shall ring for the servants to show you the door! What do you mean?"

"I mean just what I say!" and the politician's voice was angry now. "I mean that you know where your father is, and that you're only pretending you don't. It's some game to fool Reilly and me. We'll not stand for it. I want you to tell me where your father is!"

He took a step toward Grace. She seemed dazed.

"Tell me! Do you hear!" and, probably because he was so excited, the politician made a movement as if he meant to grasp the frightened girl by the arm.

"Oh!" she screamed. "Don't touch me! Larry!"

"Quit that!" cried the young reporter, stepping suddenly from behind the curtain. "That will do, Mr. Sullivan!"

Larry spoke more calmly than he had any idea he could under the circumstances. He seemed master of the situation.

The very suddenness of Larry's appearance caused Sullivan to recoil a step. He fairly glared at the young reporter and then looked at Grace, who was trembling from the words and actions of her rude visitor.

"You here!" exclaimed the politician, in a whisper. "So that's the game, eh? I thought the *Leader* was in on it."

"There's no game at all!" cried Larry, indignantly. "I am here in the interests of the paper to learn all I can about Mr. Potter's disappearance."

"Then ask her to tell you the truth!" cried Sullivan, pointing his finger at Grace. "She knows where he is!"

"I don't! I wish I did!" and Grace faced her accuser with flashing eyes.

"Don't repeat that remark," said Larry, calmly, though there was a determined air about him. "You know better than that, Mr. Sullivan," and Larry stood fearlessly before the politician. In the unlikely event of a physical encounter Larry had no fears, for he was tall and strong for his age.

"It's true!" Sullivan repeated, in a sort of a growl, for he was a little afraid of the tempest he had stirred up.

"I say it isn't," Larry replied. "I have worked on this case from the start, and I know as much about it as any one. What's more, I think you know more than you are willing to admit. I haven't forgotten the interview you gave me, and which you denied later. I think there's something under all this that will make interesting reading when it comes out."

"You—you don't suspect me, do you?" and Larry noted that Sullivan's hands were trembling.

"I don't know what to suspect," the young reporter answered, determined to take all the advantage he could of the situation. "It looks very queer. It will read queerer still when it comes out in the *Leader*—how you came here to threaten Miss Potter."

"You—you're not going to put that in, are you?" asked the politician.

"I certainly am."

"If you do I'll——"

"Look here!" exclaimed Larry. "You've made threats enough for one day. It's time for you to go. There's the door! Peterson!" he called. "Show this man out!"

Larry was rather surprised at his own assumption of authority, but Grace looked pleased.

"Yes, sir, right away, sir," replied the butler with such promptness as to indicate that he had not been far away.

He pulled back the portieres that separated the library from the hall, and stood waiting the exit of Mr. Sullivan.

"This way," he said, and a look at his portly form in comparison with the rather diminutive one of the politician would at once have prejudiced an impartial observer in favor of Peterson. "This way, if you please."

"You'll hear from me again," growled Sullivan, as he sneaked out. "I'm not done with you, Larry Dexter!"

CHAPTER XVII

GRACE GETS A LETTER

The door closed after Sullivan. Larry, standing in the library entrance, watched him leave the house. Then he turned to look at Grace.

"Oh, that was terrible!" the girl exclaimed, almost ready to cry, but bravely keeping back the tears. "What a horrid man! What did he mean?"

"I'm sure I don't know," replied Larry. "I doubt if he does himself. Mr. Potter's disappearance has evidently sent some of his plans askew, and he is hardly responsible for what he says or does. Don't let it worry you."

"I wonder if he knows where my father is?"

"I don't believe he does. If he did he would hardly come here, hoping to deceive you or your mother. No; Sullivan wants to find out where Mr. Potter is just as much as we do. Why, I can't tell yet, but he has a good reason, a strong reason, or he would not have acted as he did."

"What had I better do?" asked the girl.

"Do nothing. Leave it to me. I will write something for the *Leader* that will make Sullivan wish he had stayed away from here."

"Mother doesn't like this newspaper publicity."

"I can imagine it is not very pleasant for her," admitted Larry. "But it has to be borne if we are going to find your father. The more the papers print of the affair the better chance there is of finding him. If he is staying away for some reason he will see what a stir his disappearance has caused, and will be anxious to arrange matters so he can come back. If he is being detained against his will, the publicity will cause his captors an alarm which may result in their releasing him. So, too, if any one sees him wandering about they will recognize him by his picture, or by the description, and inform the police."

"Suppose—suppose he—should be—dead," and Grace whispered the words.

"Don't think that for a moment!"

"It is over two weeks now since he disappeared, and not one word have we heard from him."

"Persons have been known to disappear for longer periods than that, and yet turn up all right," said the young reporter, endeavoring to find some consolation for the girl. He related several instances of similar cases that had come to his attention since he had been in newspaper work.

"Now don't put too much in the paper about Mr. Sullivan—and me," said the girl as Larry was going. "There has been sufficient printed all ready, and some of my friends think I must have a staff of reporters at my beck and call, to get my name mentioned so often," and she smiled at Larry.

"I'll not mention you any more than necessary," he promised, thinking that Grace was much prettier when a smile brought out a dimple in each cheek.

Larry's description of Sullivan's visit to the Potter house proved to be what Mr. Emberg described as "a corking good scoop." None of the other papers had a line about it, of course, for Larry was the only reporter in a position to get inside information, and Sullivan was not likely to give out any account of his strange call.

"You seem to be keeping right after all the ends of this story, Larry," said Mr. Emberg the day after the account of Sullivan's visit was printed. "That's what we want. Now what sensation are you going to give us to-day?"

"I don't know. Not a very good one, I'm afraid. I've been to Mr. Potter's office. There's nothing new there, and I guess I'll have to fix up a re-hash of yesterday's stuff unless I can strike another lead. To-morrow I'm going to work on a new plan."

"What is it?" asked the city editor.

"I'm going to the steamship docks and——"

Before Larry could finish the telephone on Mr. Emberg's desk rang, and, as this instrument has precedence over everything else in a newspaper office, Larry broke off in the midst of his remark to wait until Mr. Emberg had answered the wire.

"Yes, he's here, standing right close to the 'phone," he heard the city editor say in response to the unseen questioner. "Some young lady wants to talk to you," Mr. Emberg went on, handing the portable instrument to Larry.

"Young lady to speak to me?" murmured Larry, as he took the telephone.

"This is Grace Potter," he heard through the instrument.

"Oh, how are you?" called Larry, for want of something better to say.

"Come right up," Grace said. "I have some news for you."

"What is it?"

"I have a letter from my father!"

"A letter from your father? Where is he? How did it come? Who brought it? Is he home?"

Larry fired these questions out rapidly. But there was a click in the 'phone that told him the connection was cut off. Evidently Grace had no time to tell more.

"Hurry up there!" exclaimed Mr. Emberg, as soon as he understood the import of the message Larry had received. "This will be a feature of to-day's story! Hurry, Larry!"

Larry thought the transportation facilities in New York were never so slow as on that journey to the Potter house. He tried to imagine, on the way up, what sort of a letter Grace had received from her father. That it contained good news he judged from the cheerful note in her voice.

"Things seem to be happening quite rapidly," the young reporter mused, as he got off at the elevated station nearest to his destination. "First thing I know I'll find him, and then I'll not have a chance to see Grace any more."

He dwelt on this thought, half-laughing at himself.

"I guess I'd better stop thinking of her and attend strictly to this disappearance business," he murmured as he went up the steps of the Potter mansion. "She's too rich for one thing, and another is I'm too poor, though I'm earning good wages, and we have some money in the bank," for the sale of the Bronx land, as related in "Larry Dexter, Reporter," had netted Mrs. Dexter and her children about ten thousand dollars.

Larry's ring at the bell was answered by Grace, who, it would seem, had been on the watch for him.

"I thought you would never come," she said. "I telephoned ever so long ago."

"I came as fast as I could," Larry responded. "Where is the letter?"

Grace held out to him a small piece of paper. On it was but a single line of writing. It read:

"Am well. Have to stay away for a time. Don't worry. Will write again."

It was signed with Mr. Potter's name.

"Are you sure it's from your father?" asked Larry, thinking some cruel person might be trying to play a joke, or that some enterprising reporter had sent the message for the sake of making news. Such things are sometimes done by New York newspaper men, though their city editors may know nothing about it.

"I couldn't mistake father's writing," replied Grace. "Mamma knows it is from him, and she is much happier. But we can't imagine why he has to stay away."

"When did you get this, and how did it come?" asked the reporter.

"The postman brought it a little while ago."

"Where is the envelope?"

Grace handed it to Larry. An inspection of the post-mark showed that it had been mailed in New York in the vicinity of sub-station Y, which was on the East Side. It might have been dropped in one of the many street boxes from which collections were made for that particular office, or it might have been mailed in the station itself.

"Not much to trace him by," said Larry. He looked at the envelope again and saw that there was a small ink blot on the lower left-hand corner, and that the corner where the stamp was affixed was smeared as if with some sticky substance.

"Any one would think you were a detective," said Grace, as she watched Larry examining the envelope. "What does it matter now? We are sure father is alive, for that note was posted yesterday. That has made mother and me happy. Of course we want to find him, but I don't see how you can by that letter. I thought you'd like to know about it to make a little item for the paper, and I wanted to repay you for your kindness to mother and me."

"I haven't done anything," Larry replied. "I am only too glad to be of service to you. But I may be able to find out something by this envelope."

"I don't see how."

"Will you let me take it to the sub-station?"

"Of course. But what good will that do?"

"I want to ask the sorters and clerks in charge if they remember having handled it. I may find the carrier who brought it in from the box, and he can tell in what locality it was."

"But how can they remember when they must handle thousands of letters every day?"

"Perhaps they cannot, but it is worth trying. You see in that section of the city are mostly foreigners, who write a peculiar hand, and use stationery anything but clean or of this quality. This envelope and paper are of an expensive kind."

"Yes, they are some father had made to order for his private correspondence. I did not know he took any to Europe with him, but he must have."

"It may be that a letter carrier or mail sorter took enough notice of the envelope to remember it," Larry went on. "Besides there is a small blot on it, and the way in which the stamp is put on shows that some glue or paste was applied to the envelope. Probably he used an old stamp which had no mucilage on. To make it fast to the envelope your father, or whoever posted the letter, would have had to use some sticky substance, and, in doing so, he has put it on a little too thick. Some spread out from under the stamp and soiled the envelope.

"Of course the sorters and carriers don't pay much attention to the pieces of mail, except to see that they are properly stamped and addressed, but it's worth trying. This envelope would attract attention if anything would."

"And you are going to use that for a clue?"

"I'm going to try. It may be useless. If we can find in what particular locality it was mailed we can have the police keep a watch for your father. He may mail other letters there."

"But my father is not a criminal. Why should the police watch for him so particularly. They are keeping a general lookout now, but I wouldn't like to think they were lying in wait for him."

"It's the only way to find him," said Larry. "Of course it's unpleasant, but there is evidently some mystery here, and that's the best way to clear it up."

"But he says he has to stay away for a while," argued Grace. "Maybe he wouldn't like to be found."

"Of course that point has to be considered," Larry admitted. "But I take it you and your mother want to find your father, or be in a position to communicate with him."

"Oh, we do!" exclaimed Grace.

"Then we'll have to ask the police to help us. There is no disgrace in it. Everyone knows your father is honorable, and if he wants to disappear that's his business. It is also perfectly right for you to try to find him, for——" and Larry stopped.

"Well, for what?" asked Grace, seeing the reporter hesitate.

"I don't want to alarm you," Larry went on, "but I was going to say that there is no way of telling but what some one may have imitated his writing and forged his name."

"I am sure that is my father's writing," the girl said, earnestly. "Of course I may be mistaken. I hope not. I prefer to believe that note is from him. It makes me happier."

"Of course there is only the barest possibility that this note is not from your father, but we can take no chances. That is why I want to make a systematic search, beginning at the sub-station."

"And where will it end?" asked Grace.

"I don't know. But after that I am going to the steamship piers of all the lines that ply between here and Italy."

"What for?"

"I want to see if the captain of any of the steamers recalls any man answering your father's description having come over with him. He must have sailed on some steamer, as he is in this country, if that note is from him."

"That's a good idea," commented Grace. "How I wish I could help you. Couldn't I? Couldn't I go around with you—that is to the steamer piers? I've crossed the ocean several times, and I know some of the captains of the Italian lines."

"Maybe that would be a good idea," said Larry, secretly delighted with it. "You can come with me to-morrow. I will go to the sub-station now, and will let you know what I learn. Then we will make a tour of the piers. You'll be of great assistance to me, for I know very little about steamers."

"I'm so glad!" exclaimed Grace. "It has been terrible to sit here day after day and only wait! I wanted to do something to help find father. Now there is a way! I wish I was a boy—no, I'd rather be a reporter; they can do so many things," and Grace laughed more heartily than at any time since her father had disappeared.

"I'm afraid you give us too much credit," replied Larry. "We do our best, but we don't always get results. Are you sure your mother will let you go?"

"Of course," Grace replied, in a way that showed she was used to having her own way. "When will you come for me to-morrow?"

"In the morning."

"I can hardly wait. Now don't forget. I'll be your assistant. Maybe I could learn enough to be a woman reporter some day."

"I have no doubt you could," Larry responded, as he went out on his way to the sub-station with the envelope, having telephoned to the police of the letter and securing a promise that no other reporters would be informed of it for a while.

As he walked along, his thoughts were busy in many directions. The receipt of the letter, the clues the envelope offered, the plans for a search among the ship captains, and, above all, Grace's offer to accompany him, made Larry speculate on what the Potter mystery was coming to.

"I wonder what the other fellows on the *Leader* would say if they knew I was working this assignment in company with the millionaire's daughter," said Larry to himself. "I guess I'd better not say anything about it. They'd make fun of me. I know it's all right to take her, or I wouldn't do it. Besides, if she knows the captains she can be of considerable aid to me. Queer, though, for Larry

Dexter, who used to rush copy, to be hunting for a missing millionaire in company with his pretty daughter."

It was odd, but no other line of activity is so filled with strange surprises, or brings about such a variety of work, as being a newspaper reporter of the first class.

Larry struck several snags when he attempted to get information at the sub-station. In the first place none of the officials in charge would give him any news about the envelope unless he got an order from the New York postmaster himself. The government has very strict regulations in regard to giving out information about mail matter. But Larry was not daunted. He telephoned to Mr. Emberg, and the forces of the newspaper were set to work. Certain political wires were "pulled," and, as there were on the *Leader* men to whom the postmaster was under obligations, that official gave the clerks at the sub-station permission to tell Larry whatever he wanted to know.

"Sorry we had to have so much red tape about it," the sub-station agent said, when Larry came back with the magical paper that opened the mouths of the subordinates.

"Oh, that's all right," the reporter said. "I know how it is. Now, what I want to know is, in what box was that letter posted?" and he held out the envelope Grace had given him.

"Rather hard to say," spoke the head clerk. "I'll show it to all the carriers who are in now, and later to those who come in during the afternoon. They may recognize it. It's a little out of the run of ordinary envelopes we get in this section of the city."

One after another several carriers scanned the envelope. All shook their heads, until it came to an elderly man. As soon as he saw the envelope he exclaimed:

"I brought that in. I remember it very well." "Where did you get it?" asked Larry, eagerly. "A man gave it to me last night, just as I was taking the mail from a box down near the river," was the unexpected reply.

CHAPTER XVIII

LARRY IS BAFFLED

This was much better than Larry had expected. To have the envelope remembered so soon was good, but to have the carrier who brought it in say he recalled having received it from the person who mailed the letter, was better yet.

"What sort of a man was he?" asked Larry, his heart beating high with hope.

"Why do you ask?" inquired the carrier.

"I'm a reporter from the *Leader*, and I'm trying to locate Mr. Potter, the missing millionaire," said Larry. "This letter was from him."

"Then I can't be of much service to you," the postman went on. "This was given to me by a man who bore no resemblance to Mr. Potter, whose picture I have lately seen in the papers."

"But what sort of a looking man gave you this envelope?" asked Larry.

"He was a smooth-shaven man, rather poorly dressed. I'll tell you how it was. This box, at which I was when the man gave me the letter, is at the foot of a street leading to the river. It is the last one I collect from at night. I had taken out all the mail in the box, and was just locking it up again when some one came up the street in a hurry. I looked around, for the neighborhood is a lonely one, and, as I did so, I saw a man come to a halt, as if he was surprised to see me at the box. I could see he had a letter in his hand.

"'Come on,' I said, for often people run up to me at the last minute to have me take letters. 'Come on,' I said, for I was in a hurry. 'I'll take the letter.'

"At that the man pulled his hat down over his eyes and advanced slowly. He held the letter out to me, and, as he did so, I caught a glimpse of his face, as the light from a street lamp flashed on it. I could see he was smooth shaven. I took the letter and put it in my bag. As I did so the man seemed to melt away in the shadows. I thought it rather queer at the time, for it seemed as if the fellow was afraid I'd recognize him. But I'd never seen him before, so far as I know, so he needn't have been alarmed. I brought the letter to the office, and as I sorted my mail, I noted that the stamp had been stuck on with plenty of mucilage. I also saw the blot, and, as the envelope was unlike any I had ever seen before, as far as size and quality of paper went, the thing was impressed on my mind.

"That's all I know about it," the carrier finished, "but I'm sure the man who gave me the letter was not the missing millionaire. I've seen his picture too many times lately to be mistaken."

"Then who could it have been?" asked Larry.

"That's a hard question, young man," said the carrier. "It might have been any one else. I think it was a person who didn't care about being seen, and didn't want to attract any attention. I guess he would have been better satisfied to have dropped the letter in the box when no one was looking, but seeing me there he came up with it before he knew what he was doing."

"If the letter was from Mr. Potter, and it wasn't the millionaire who mailed it, he must have got some one to do it," the chief clerk of the sub-station suggested, and Larry was forced to adopt this idea. He inquired as to the location of the box at which the carrier stood when he received the missive, and asked in what direction the man came from. Having learned these facts, and deciding he could gain nothing more by staying longer at the sub-station, Larry hurried to the *Leader* office.

"Well, I've gained something," he said to himself. "I've got a good story, and I have a slender clue to work on. I must write the story first, however. Then I'll go back and tell Grace what I learned."

The account of the letter and the circumstances under which it was mailed created a new sensation in the Potter mystery, and, as on several other occasions, the *Leader* scored a beat.

As soon as he had finished the story Larry went to see Grace, whom he found anxiously waiting for him. She asked a score of questions as to what he had learned, and the reporter told her all about his trip to the sub-station.

"What are you going to do next?" she inquired.

"I think I'll go over on the East Side and make some inquiries. Your father may be staying there," answered Larry.

Going downtown in an elevated train, and taking a stroll through that populous section, known as the "East Side," Larry soon found himself in the neighborhood of the box at which the carrier had received the letter written by Mr. Potter. He took a brief survey of the locality.

"Not very promising," was his mental comment.

All about were big tenement houses of a substantial kind. They were built of brick, and from nearly every window a woman's head protruded, while the street swarmed with children. It was a neighborhood teeming with life, for it was the abode of the poor, and they were quartered together almost like rabbits in a warren.

For want of something better to do, Larry strolled down one side of the street, at the end of which was located the letter box which formed such a slender clue. Then he walked up the other side, looking about him idly, in vain hopes of stumbling on something that would put him on the track.

It was late in the afternoon, and the streets were beginning to fill with workers hurrying home, for the day's labor was over. As Larry strolled along, rather careless of his steps, he collided with a man in front of a big tenement building.

"Excuse me," murmured the reporter.

"I beg your pardon," the man said, grabbing hold of Larry to prevent them both from falling, so forceful had been the impact. "I was looking to see if my wife was watching for me. She generally looks out of the window to see me coming down the street, and then she puts the potatoes on."

"I guess I wasn't looking where I was going," said Larry, as he disengaged himself from the man's grip. "I was—why, hello, Mr. Jackson!" he exclaimed.

"What! Why, bless my soul if it isn't Larry Dexter!" and the man held out his hand. "Why, I haven't seen you in a long time. How's your mother and the children?"

"Fine. How's Mrs. Jackson?"

"She's well. There she is looking out of the window, wondering why I don't come home to supper. You must come in and see her. Come, and stay to supper."

The man Larry had thus unexpectedly met was the one in whose flat Mrs. Dexter and the children had stayed the first night they had come to New York, and found that the sister of Larry's mother, with whom they expected to remain, had suddenly moved away. The Dexter family, sad and discouraged at the loss of their farm, would have fared badly on their arrival in the big city had not Mrs. Jackson and her husband befriended them.

While Larry was getting a start in the newspaper work the Dexter family had lived in the same tenement with the Jacksons, and they had become firm friends. Larry and his mother since then had moved to other quarters, and had, for some time back, lost trace of their acquaintances.

"I didn't know you lived here," said Larry when he had recovered somewhat from his surprise at seeing Mr. Jackson.

"We haven't lived here long. I got a better position in this part of the city, and as I like to be near my work I moved here. We like it quite well, but it's rather crowded. However, almost any place is in New York. But you must come in to supper. Mrs. Jackson will be anxious to hear all about your folks. I can see her making signs to me to hurry up. I suppose the potatoes are all cooked and the tea made."

Larry did not require much urging to accept the kind invitation. He wanted to see his friends again, and he thought they might be able to give him some information concerning the people of the neighborhood.

"Because it's the best place in the world to hide in. If I wanted to drop out of sight I'd go about two blocks away from here and keep quiet. No one would ever think of looking for me so near my home."

"I hope you don't contemplate anything like that," said Larry with a laugh.

"No, indeed. But New York is the best hiding place, and you can depend on it, Mr. Potter is here."

"You haven't seen him in the neighborhood, have you?" asked the reporter, glad of the opportunity which gave him a chance for that question.

"No, I can't say that I have. If they'd offer a reward I might take time to hunt for him," and Mr. Jackson laughed. "I can't afford to turn detective as it is now," he added. "It's too hard to get a living."

Larry spent the evening with his friends, keeping the talk as much as possible, without exciting suspicion, on the Potter case. In this way he learned considerable about the persons living in the immediate vicinity of the Jacksons, for Mrs. Jackson was fond of making new acquaintances.

But in all this there was no clue such as Larry sought. There were any number of men, concerning whom there seemed to be some mystery, but none answered the description of Mr. Potter.

"There are a queer lot of people in this tenement," said Mr. Jackson, during the course of the talking. "All of 'em have some story hidden away, I guess. Especially one man."

"Who is he?"

"Nobody knows," replied Mr. Jackson. "He came here one night, and seemed quite excited. Let's see, it was Thursday night, I remember now. He acted as though he was afraid some one was after him."

"Thursday night," thought Larry. "That was the night the man got away from the deserted tenement."

"My wife and I were sitting here," continued Mr. Jackson, "when all at once a knock sounded on the door. I opened it, and there was this man. He asked if I had any rooms to rent. I hadn't, but I told him I had a spare bed, for I saw he was respectable. He seemed glad to get it, and paid me well, though I didn't want to take the money. But he seemed to have plenty."

"What was queer about him?" asked Larry, beginning to take an unusual interest in what his friend was saying.

"Well, the excitement he seemed to be in, for one thing. And another, he had just been shaved. I could see the talcum powder on his cheeks. I thought it strange that a man who had time to shave or get shaved should be in such a hurry. But it wasn't any of my affair, so I said nothing."

"What became of him?" Larry was quite eager now. He seemed to be on the verge of discovering something; if not of the Potter mystery then of the other, that cropped up every now and again—that of the man he had helped save from the wreck.

"He went away the next morning," Mr. Jackson resumed. "I didn't see him again until the next night. Then he told me he had a room in this tenement."

"Where?" inquired the young reporter.

"On the floor below—a front room, at the end of the corridor. But are you going to call on him?" and Mr. Jackson looked somewhat surprised at Larry's eagerness.

"Maybe I could get a story out of him," replied the reporter non-commitally. "Have to be always on the lookout, you know."

"Well, I guess you'll not get much out of this man," said Mr. Jackson. "He hardly speaks to me, though he doesn't seem cross or ugly. Only there's some mystery about him. I'm sure of that."

"If he's Mah Retto I'm positive there is," thought Larry. "And it looks as if it might be that fellow."

Not wishing to seem too keen on the scent of the queer man, the newspaper youth changed the subject. In a little while he said he had better be going home, as he had not told his mother he would be out late. He promised to ask Mrs. Dexter to call on Mrs. Jackson, and, with many good wishes from his friends, he left.

"Now for a try at the room on the next floor," said Larry in a whisper, as he found himself in the corridor. "It's only a slim chance, but a reporter has to take all that come his way."

He found the room Mr. Jackson had described, and knocked on the door. There was a sound from within, as though some one had arisen from a chair. Then a voice asked:

"Who's there?"

"Does Mah Retto live here?" asked Larry, determining on a bold plan.

Hardly had he spoken the words when the door was quickly opened.

CHAPTER XIX

GRACE ON THE TRAIL

Larry saw, standing before him, framed in the doorway from which streamed the glare from a big reading lamp, the man of mystery—the fellow who had escaped from the tumble-down tenement—the man he and Bailey had pulled ashore on the life-raft.

"Are you Mah Retto?" asked Larry again, rather at a loss for something to say, when he saw the strange man confronting him.

The mysterious one looked at Larry for several seconds. He seemed much excited, and in doubt as to what to do. Then, seeming to arrive at a sudden decision, he quickly closed the door, and Larry heard the key turned in the lock.

"Not much satisfaction in that," muttered the young reporter. "That was him, though. I wonder what I had better do?"

Larry stood in the hallway, undecided. He wanted another opportunity to see and speak to the man he believed was Mah Retto, but he considered it would not be wise to knock again on the door. The occupant of the room either would not answer or would order him away.

"I'll have to come again," Larry said to himself. "I've learned one thing, anyhow, and that is where he lives."

The young reporter went to the office of the *Leader* early the next morning. He found Mr. Emberg on hand, and told the city editor the plans for the day; that of making a tour of the steamship piers. Mr. Emberg thought this was a good idea, and complimented Larry on his work thus far.

"I ran across my old friend, the East Indian, last night," Larry said, as he was leaving. "I'm going to work him up for a story when I get through with this Potter case."

"Don't do it until then," advised Mr. Emberg. "I want you to devote all your attention to the missing millionaire. The East Indian story will not amount to much or I'd put another man on it. You may get a yarn for the Saturday supplement out of it, but even that's doubtful."

Larry thought differently, but he did not say so. Nor did he mention that he was going to take Grace Potter with him on his tour of the docks. He had an idea that the city editor might object, or laugh at him, and Larry did not care to have that happen. He felt he was doing right, and he knew there could be no serious objection to the daughter of the missing man aiding in a search for her parent.

Larry found Grace waiting for him. She was quietly dressed, and wore a heavy veil, so that no one in the street would recognize her, since her picture had been published in several papers, and there might be comments from the crowd if the daughter of Mr. Potter was seen out in company of a newspaper reporter.

"Anything new?" asked the young lady, for she had taken to greeting Larry in that newspaper fashion.

"Not much. I didn't learn anything of consequence by my trip to the East Side last night. I'm not done there, however. Now we'll try the piers, and see what sort of a 'pull' you have with the captains of the vessels."

"We may not find many captains," Grace said, "unless their ships are about to sail. Still it is worth trying. Shall we start?"

"I'm ready any time you are," Larry answered. "What did your mother say?"

"She objected a bit at first, but I soon convinced her it was for the best."

Larry thought it would not have been hard for Grace to have convinced him that almost anything was for the best. She looked quite trim in her dark dress, with her glossy hair held snugly in place by her veil.

As they went down the steps of the mansion Larry saw a man, who was standing on the other side of the street, move rapidly away, as if he had been watching the house. The young reporter uttered an exclamation before he was aware of it, and Grace quickly asked:

"What's the matter?"

"I—I saw some one," Larry replied.

"Any one would think it was a ghost from the way you act," the girl went on, with a little laugh. She was in much better spirits than any time since her father had disappeared, for the chance of helping to search for him, and the change, from sitting idly in the house waiting for news, was a welcome relief.

"No, it wasn't a ghost. It was a man I'd like to have a chance to talk to," Larry went on.

"Would he give you—er—a 'story'? Is that what you call it?"

"That's right. Yes, I believe he could give me a story," and Larry looked in the direction the man had gone. He was no longer to be seen. "A very good story," he added, for the man was the same one he had surprised in the tenement the night before—the man of the life-raft.

However, he could not leave Grace to go in search of the strange individual, and it was more important, as Mr. Emberg had said, to stick to the Potter case. The other could wait.

"All the same I'd like to know what he was doing in this neighborhood," thought Larry. He puzzled over the matter for several seconds as he and Grace went along.

On the way downtown the two discussed their plans. There were not many Italian steamship lines to visit, but it might take some time to see the captains of all the boats at present in port.Some of the commanders would be at their hotels pending the loading of their vessels.

"Have you made up your mind what you want to ask them?" inquired Larry, as they were nearing the station where they intended to get off.

"What I want principally to know is if a person answering my father's description came over with them lately. I want to find out, in case he did, how he acted, and if he gave any hint of being in trouble."

"That may be a good clue to follow," Larry sad. "Now we'll make our first attempt."

It ended in failure, for though they found the captain of the Italian steamer they boarded in the cabin of his vessel, he could not aid them. He was very polite about it, and seemed quite sorry that he could be of no service.

It was the same in a number of other cases. Some of the captains remembered Grace, for she had crossed with them once or twice, but none of them recalled a man answering Mr. Potter's description making the voyage with them recently.

The last place they visited was the dock of the line to which the wrecked *Olivia* belonged. This line Grace had never traveled on, but she had a letter of introduction to the manager from the captain of the *Messina*, on which she had made her last trip. The commanders of two steamers of this company were in port. One of them was at the dock, for his vessel was about to sail.

To him Grace made her inquiries, but fruitlessly. She turned away, rather disappointed. There was but one more chance left. The other captain was at his hotel, not far away, for seamen like to remain near the water front.

"We'll go there," said Larry, "and then I must get back to the office, and write my story for to-day's paper."

"I wish you had some better news," spoke Grace. "But I am afraid Captain Padduci, whom we are now going to see, will prove as disappointing as the rest."

"We'll hope for the best," remarked Larry. "I wish——"

But what he wished he never told, for at that instant his attention was attracted by a voice. It was that of a man who stood at the small window of the steamship office. The window was one which he and Grace had just stepped away from, after inquiring as to where Captain Padduci's hotel was.

If the voice attracted Larry the sight of the man himself did more to rivet his attention. For the first glance showed him the inquirer was none other than the mysterious individual, Mah Retto.

"I would like to inquire where I can find Captain Tantrella of the steamer *Olivia*," the man asked of the clerk.

"The *Olivia* is lost," replied the steamship clerk.

"I know it, but I would like to see the captain. He was saved, I believe."

"Yes, he was. He commands a freight ship now. She's due in port in a few days. The *Turtle* is her name. You can come around when she gets in."

The mysterious man turned away as though disappointed. As he did so he caught sight of Larry, and instantly he hurried out of the office.

Larry was greatly excited. He was convinced, more than ever, that there was something in this man's actions that made him an object of suspicion. He felt that he must follow the fellow, but he could not leave Grace. He looked around for her, but she had gone to the ladies' dressing room to adjust her veil and hat, which had been blown about by the high wind. She came back presently, to find Larry much agitated.

"What is the matter?" she asked.

"Nothing much," replied Larry. "I just saw my queer stranger again and——"

"You'd like to follow him, and you don't want to leave me," put in Grace with quick wit. "Now run right along. I can go to that hotel all by myself and see Captain Padduci. I'm not a bit afraid. I once traveled from London to Paris alone. You hurry after him, and I'll see the captain. I'll telephone you the result of my interview. You can come up and see me this evening, and we'll talk over some more plans."

"That will be good," Larry said, "but are you sure you won't mind me leaving you?"

"I can get along all right," replied Grace. "Of course I'd like to have you come along, for I believe you understand this matter better than I do, but I want you to find that other man and get your story."

Larry was inclined both ways, but he knew it would be better to hurry after Mah Retto, as Grace could make all the necessary inquiries of Captain Padduci.

"Until to-night, then," the young reporter said, as he hurried out of the steamship office, and Grace turned to go to the captain's hotel.

Reaching the street Larry saw, some distance ahead of him, the form of the man whose actions so puzzled him, and who had led him such a baffling chase.

"Here is where I get you," thought Larry, as he hurried on.

CHAPTER XX

LARRY GETS A SCARE

Through the crowded street the young reporter ran, bumping into several persons, and causing them to mutter more or less impolite exclamations about youths who trod on the toes of innocent pedestrians.

Larry could catch occasional glimpses of his man, and he noted that Retto looked back every now and then to see if he was being followed.

"Oh, I'm after you, my East Indian friend," Larry remarked to himself. "I'm going to have an accounting with you now. There's something queer about you."

No sooner had Larry given expression to this last sentence, speaking somewhat aloud, as was his habit when thinking intently, than he slipped on a banana pealing and fell down with a force that jarred him all over.

"I'll have to be more careful," thought Larry, as he got up and found that no bones were broken. He started off again after Retto. "I wasn't looking where I was going, thinking so much of Retto. Where is he now? He must have got quite a way ahead."

He had; so far that Larry could no longer see him. The reporter tried to peer through the ever-shifting crowd, for a glimpse of Retto, but with no success.

"He's gone," he murmured. "However, I know where he lives and I'll go there at once. No! I've got to get a story in for to-day's paper about Mr. Potter. I haven't much time before the first edition. Guess I'd better telephone it in, and let Mr. Emberg have one of the men fix it up."

In his eagerness to catch Retto, Larry had rather lost sight of his more important duties, and, as he looked at his watch, he found he had no time to spare if the *Leader* was to have a story that day.

He looked for the blue sign, indicating a public telephone station, and saw one a few doors down the street. On his way there he ran over in his mind the points of the story. It would be based on the search and inquiry among the steamship captains.

"I've got to say it resulted in nothing," Larry remarked to himself. "Hold on, though. Suppose Grace gets a clue from Captain Padduci? I'll be in a pretty mess if she does, and I telephone in that we found out nothing. Wish I hadn't chased after that East Indian. I should have stayed with Grace until we got through.

"No help for it, though. So here goes. I wish I'd done as Mr. Emberg said and let the Retto matter drop. But it seemed too good to lose sight of."

He soon had the *Leader* office on the wire, and, a few seconds later, was talking to Mr. Emberg. He was rather surprised at what the city editor said.

"What's the matter with you, Larry?" was the inquiry that came through the telephone. "We've been waiting for you. Have you seen the *Scorcher*?"

"No. Why?" asked Larry, an uneasy feeling coming over him. There seemed an atmosphere of "beat" about him, and he was afraid of Mr. Emberg's next words.

"Why, they've got a big story about Mr. Potter being home," went on the city editor. "They say he is concealed in the house, and has been ever since the scare."

"That's not true!" replied Larry. "I was at the house this morning, and he wasn't home. I've been all around the steamer piers and got no trace of him. I just left his daughter, and she would know if he had been home all this while."

"Well, they've got the story," repeated Mr. Emberg, with the insistence that city editors sometimes use when they fear their reporters have been beaten. "I sent Harvey up to the house in a hurry to make inquiries. The *Scorcher* got out an extra. Where have you been?"

"I just finished the tour of the docks."

"Well, you'd better go up to the house and make sure. It looks queer."

"I'll bet that story came from Sullivan," said Larry. "He's sore on us, and would do anything to get even. He wants to find Mr. Potter, you know."

"I hope you're right," and Mr. Emberg's voice was not as cordial as it usually was. "Let me hear from you soon again. I'll have one of the men fix up something for the first edition. You tell him about the inquiries made of the ship captains."

Larry's heart was like lead. To have worked so hard, and then to have another paper come out with a "scare" story about Mr. Potter's return, was discouraging.

"That story's a fake," he decided, as he prepared to telephone in the result of his morning's work. "I'll prove it is, too, and make them take back-water."

Larry's story of the trip to the steamship offices was not very interesting reading, for it was but a record of failure. He realized that, but there was nothing else to print and the paper had to have something. It was not Larry's fault, for even a reporter on a special assignment cannot provide fresh and startling news every day, though all newspaper men try hard enough for this desirable end.

After Larry had telephoned in all the information he had, he hurried uptown to the Potter house. He found Grace had just come in, and, to Larry's relief, she had not been successful in getting any news from Captain Padduci. In a few words the reporter told what the *Scorcher* had printed.

"We must deny that at once!" exclaimed Grace. "I wonder why they print such untruths!"

"For one reason, because the *Scorcher* is trying to live up to its name and give the public 'hot' news," replied Larry, "and, for another, because Sullivan has some end to gain. He stands in with the *Scorcher* men, and I think my old enemy, Peter Manton, is responsible for this."

"What can you do to offset it?" asked Grace.

"I can have a signed statement from you or your mother in our last edition."

"A signed statement?"

"Yes, a little interview with you, in the form of a communication, with your name at the foot, denying that your father is at home. This will take the wind out of the *Scorcher's* sails."

"Then I'll give you the interview at once. What shall I say?"

Larry told her, and in a few minutes the message was being dictated over the Potter telephone to Mr. Emberg.

"I'm glad to hear this, Larry," the city editor said. "We had quite a scare. I thought they had you beaten, even though Harvey came back and said Mrs. Potter sent down word there was no truth in the *Scorcher* yarn. You certainly had us scared."

"I was frightened myself," admitted Larry, with a laugh.

"This will make story enough for to-day, unless you find Mr. Potter," Mr. Emberg went on. "Now lay pipes for something for to-morrow."

"I will," Larry replied, though he did not in the least know what new features he could "play up."

At that instant the bell rang, and a whistle indicated that the letter carrier was at the door. Grace answered it. She came back on the run, a missive in her hand.

"It's from my father!" she exclaimed, as she tore open the envelope.

Larry watched Grace while she read the letter. It was short, for she had quickly finished with it and turned to the reporter.

"He's written about you!" she exclaimed.

"About me?"

"Yes. Listen," and Grace read:

"'I am well. Still have to remain away. Don't try to find me. Will be home soon. Tell Larry Dexter to give up. He's chasing me too close.'"

"Chasing him too close!" exclaimed Larry in bewilderment. I only wish I was! I haven't the least clue to his whereabouts. I wonder what he means? Is that his writing?"

"I can't be mistaken in that," Grace replied. "It is just the same as the other letter was."

"Let me see," and the young reporter examined the envelope. It was similar to that containing the first note which had come from Mr. Potter, save there was no blot on it and the stamp showed no excess of mucilage.

"I'll take this to the sub-station," Larry went on. "It was probably mailed in the same place as was the other. I'll see if the carrier had any such experience as he did with the former note."

"I think it would be a good plan," Grace answered. "Oh, this is beginning to wear on my nerves! As for mother, she is almost ill over it. Her physician says if father is not found soon he cannot say what will happen to mother."

"Still she must know your father is safe."

"That is the worst of it. She will not believe these notes are from him, or, rather, she believes he is held captive somewhere and is forced to write them. Nothing I can say will make her think differently. She is wearing herself to a shadow over it."

"We must do something!" exclaimed Larry.

"Yes; but what?" asked the girl. "You are working hard and I am doing all I can, but our efforts seem to amount to nothing. What more can we do?"

"I'm trying to think of a plan," Larry responded. "The search of the steamship piers gave us no clue; the police here have not been able to find a trace. We can try one thing more."

"What is that?"

"You can hire private detectives. Sometimes, in cases of this kind, they are better than the police, as they assign one man, who devotes all his attention to the search, while the police, as a rule, don't bother much to find missing persons."

"Then I'll hire the best private detectives to be had!" exclaimed Grace. "Where ought I to go?"

Larry named an agency, that he had heard was first-class, and offered to take Grace to the office. The reporter knew one of the men on the staff, as he had once written a story in which he figured, and the officer had been grateful for the mention of his name. Detectives, even private ones, are prone to vanity in this respect, as a rule.

"I don't like to take up so much of your time," objected the girl, as Larry prepared to go with her to the detective agency.

"My time is yours in this case. I have nothing to do for the *Leader* but to find your father. This is part of the work."

"I wouldn't think it could pay a newspaper to put one man exclusively on a case like this."

"The editors think it does. In the first place it makes some news every day, and the papers have to have news. Then if I should happen to find Mr. Potter, it would be a big advertisement for the *Leader*, and that is what all the New York papers are looking for. The better advertised they are the better prices they can charge for the advertisements printed in them, for it's from theadvertisements that a newspaper makes its money. Besides, I've promised to find your father for you and I'm going to do it!" Larry looked very determined.

"My! I never supposed newspaper work was so complicated," said Grace, with a little sigh. "Now let's go to the detectives. I'm almost afraid. It sounds so awful to say 'detective.'"

Larry found the man he knew in the office of the agency, and the latter introduced him to the chief. The reporter explained the reason for the visit, and Grace added a plea that they do all in their power to locate Mr. Potter.

"I thought you'd come here sooner or later," said the chief with a smile. "Most folks do when they find the regular police don't give enough attention to the cases. It's not the fault of the police, though. They have so much to do they can't give much time to a single case. But of course we can. Now then, tell me all about it."

Which Grace, aided by Larry, proceeded to do. The chief listened intently, and asked several questions. He took the two letters which Grace had from her father and looked carefully at them.

"Do you think you'll be able to do anything?" asked the girl anxiously. The strain was beginning to tell heavily on her.

"Of course we will!" exclaimed the chief, heartily. "We'll find your father for you, you can depend on it!"

Larry did not want to tell her that the chief was thus optimistic in regard to every case he undertook. It was a habit of his, not a bad one, perhaps, and it did little harm, for nearly all of his clients wanted cheering up.

"What do you think about this, young man?" asked the chief, turning suddenly to Larry.

"In regard to what, Mr. Grover?"

"Where do you think Mr. Potter is? I understand you've been working on this case. In fact, I have all your stories clipped from the *Leader*."

Larry had not forgotten about Retto, and he determined to pay the fellow another visit.

With him, to think was to act. He soon found himself going up the stairs of the tenement house, and presently reached Retto's door. His knock brought no response, and he stood for a moment, undecided what to do. Then a bold idea came to him.

"I'll try the door and see if he's home," he said. "If he isn't, there's no harm done. If he is, I can explain it somehow."

Larry, after a moment's hesitation to listen for any possible movement on the other side of the portal, tried the door. It opened easily for him, though it needed but a glance to show that the apartment was empty and vacated. All the furniture was gone.

"He's skipped!" exclaimed Larry, as he struck a match and looked around. "I guess he was afraid I'd find him. Well, I am more determined than ever that I'll land this man. I wonder if he left any clues behind?"

He lighted a jet of a wall fixture, for the gas had not been shut off. In the glare he saw a scrap of paper lying on the floor. He picked it up. As he glanced at it he gave a cry of astonishment.

"Who would have thought it!" exclaimed Larry to himself. "Of all the strange things! I wonder I didn't connect him with the case before! This explains why he was in front of the house."

For, the paper he had picked up was part of an envelope like those which had contained the letters Grace received from her father. And on the scrap was her name, but the envelope had been spoiled by a blot of ink in writing the address. It had been torn up and thrown away, to remain a mute bit of evidence.

"Mah Retto knows Mr. Potter!" exclaimed Larry. "Retto is the man who mailed the letters for the missing millionaire. If I find him I can make him tell me where Mr. Potter is! Now to trace my mysterious East Indian friend!"

CHAPTER XXI

TRACING RETTO

Larry took another survey of the apartment to see if there were any more clues that might aid him. But the one that had so unexpectedly come to his hand was all he found. The place showed evidences of having been hastily vacated.

"I'll see Mr. Jackson," he decided. "Perhaps he can tell me something. He was interested in this queer man."

He lost no time in going to the rooms of his friends. They were glad to see him, and asked a number of questions about his mother, sisters and brother. But Larry, as soon as he could, turned the subject to Retto.

"He's gone," he told Mr. Jackson.

"I supposed he had. I saw the janitor taking his things from the room this morning."

"Do you know where he went to?" asked the young reporter eagerly. "I want to find him."

"I haven't the least idea."

"I wonder if the janitor would know," Larry went on.

"He might. Perhaps the man left his address with him, in order that letters might be forwarded. I'll go downstairs with you and introduce you to the janitor."

That functionary was unable to throw any light on where Retto had gone. Evidently, for the time being, the chase had come to an end.

Larry made his way to the nearest elevated station and rode in the direction of the Potter home. He had no definite plan in mind, and, more from a whim than anything else, he decided to walk past the house. He did not expect it, but he had an idea—a very faint one—that he might see Grace. Of course, if he saw her at the window, where she sometimes sat, it would be no more than polite to go in and tell her what the carrier had said about the second letter.

When Larry got in front of the Potter house he was disappointed to see that it was in darkness. It was about ten o'clock, and he knew the family was in the habit of retiring early, especially since Mr. Potter's disappearance.

As he strolled past on the other side of the street, looking in vain for a glimmer of light, or the sight of a girlish face against the window pane, he passed into the deep shadow cast by a big tree on which shone an electric arc light in front of the Potter house. The blackness was quite deep, in contrast to the illumination on both sides of the tree, for electric lamps have the property of casting dense shadows. If Larry had been looking straight in front of him perhaps it would not have happened, but he was staring at where Grace lived, and the first thing he knew he had walked full tilt into a man who was hiding in the darkness behind the big tree.

"Oh—ugh!" grunted Larry, for the breath was knocked from his body by the sudden impact.

"What's the matter? What are you doing?" inquired the man angrily. "Why don't you look where you're going?"

The collision had swung him out of the shadow into the light, where he stood blinking. Larry recovered his breath, and then, at the sight of the man, gave a low-voiced cry of astonishment.

"Mr. Sullivan!" he exclaimed.

"Oh, it's you, is it, Dexter!" remarked the politician. "Are you following me? Are you spying on me? If you are I'll have you arrested!"

"I'm not following you or spying on you!" retorted Larry. "But you seem to be hiding here. What do you want? What are you in front of Mr. Potter's house for?"

He was determined to follow up his advantage, and to show Sullivan that he was not in the least intimidated by him. Clearly there was something in the wind when the district political leader was hiding behind trees watching the house of the missing millionaire.

"Look here!" exclaimed Sullivan, and he had moved back until he was in the shadow. "You go along and mind your own business; do you hear? Move along now!"

"I guess I have as good a right as you have to remain on the street. And this sidewalk is just as public as any in New York, even if it is in the millionaire section. What are you hiding for? Do you expect to see Mr. Potter come walking down the steps? If you do I'll wait, too. I'd like to see him."

"You think you're very smart because you're a reporter," retorted Sullivan, becoming more and more angry as he saw he could not intimidate Larry. "Let me tell you you're making a big mistake. I have some power in New York, and I warn you that I'll use it if you don't stop interfering with me. You've made me trouble enough. Now you be off, or I'll call a policeman and have you arrested."

"You can't," replied Larry. "I haven't done anything except to run into you, and that was an accident, caused by you being in the shadow."

"I'll show you what I can do. The police of this district know me, and they'll do anything I say."

"You might have 'pull' enough to have me arrested," Larry admitted, "but I wouldn't stay locked up long. A telephone message to the city editor of the *Leader*, and a word from him to some one higher up than a policeman, would bring about a change. And I don't think you'd like to read the story in the paper the next day, Mr. Sullivan."

The politician was silent. He knew Larry had the best of the argument. For, though the Assembly leader had some power in New York, he was only a "small fry" when it came to an important matter, such as he knew would result if Larry was taken into custody. He contented himself, therefore, with growling out threats against Larry in particular and all newspaper men in general.

"You'll interfere with me once too often," said Sullivan. "I warn you, young man. You're making a big mistake. There's more behind this matter than you have any idea of."

"I know there is," replied Larry quickly. "That's why I'm working so hard to clear up the mystery. I want to find out what your part is in the disappearance of Mr. Potter."

"My part? What do you mean?"

"You know well enough what I mean. You are interested in Mr. Potter. You want him to come back. Now what for? Has it anything to do with the new line? Does it concern your friends, Kilburn and Reilly? That's what I want to know and what I'm going to find out. You're playing a deep game, Mr. Sullivan, but I'll beat you at it!"

Larry was quite surprised at his own eloquence, and the manner in which he bid defiance to the leader of the assembly district.

"Hush!" exclaimed the politician. "If you say another word I'll knock you down!" and he advanced toward Larry as though he intended to carry the threat into execution. "Keep quiet, I say!"

"Are you afraid of having the truth told?" asked Larry speaking a little louder. It seemed that Sullivan was worried lest some one might overhear the talk. The streets, however, were deserted at this time.

"Never you mind!" retorted Sullivan. "You've said enough, so that I'll not forget it in a hurry, and Jack Sullivan is a bad man to have for an enemy, let me tell you."

"I don't doubt that, but I'm not afraid of you. I believe you know something of Mr. Potter's disappearance, and I'm going to find out what it is. You are waiting here with some object in view, and I'm going to discover it."

"Get away from here!" ordered Sullivan, hardly able to speak because of his anger.

"I'm going to stay as long as I like."

"Move on!" exclaimed the politician. "Get away or——"

He emerged from the shadow and approached Larry. The man's face showed how wrought up he was, and though he was not much taller or stronger than Larry he had a man's energy, and would prove more than a match for the lad if it came to a fight. And it looked now as though he was going to resort to desperate measures in order to accomplish his ends.

"I'm going to stay until I see what you're up to!" said Larry firmly, bracing himself to meet the expected attack.

Sullivan doubled up his fists and drew nearer to the youth. He raised his arm, as though to strike. The two were beyond the shadow of the tree now, and in plain view.

Sullivan's fist shot out, but Larry was watching and cleverly dodged it. The politician overreached himself, lost his balance, and, his fist meeting nothing more solid than air, he pitched forward and fell on the sidewalk.

Larry swung around, ready to meet his opponent when he should come back to the attack. At that instant a window, in a house across the street, opened, and a voice the young reporter knew was Grace's called:

"Larry! Larry! Come here!"

He started to run across the thoroughfare, but, as he did so, he saw another man emerge from behind a tree, next to the one where Sullivan had been concealed. And, as the light from an arc lamp gleamed on this man's face, Larry saw it was that of Mah Retto.

The young reporter paused, undecided what to do. Across the street he could see Grace in the raised window, waiting for him—for what he did not know. But, even as he looked at her, he saw Retto running off down the street. In an instant Larry's mind was made up. He took after Retto as fast as he could run.

CHAPTER XXII

GRACE IS SUSPICIOUS

Retto headed for Central Park, and as Larry saw him pass the entrance he realized that it was going to be as hard to follow the man as though he had disappeared in the midst of a crowd, especially since the park was not well lighted.

"But I've got to follow him," thought Larry. "It's my best chance. I must find out where he has moved to. I wonder what Grace wanted? And I wonder what Sullivan's game was? My, but the questions are coming too thick for me. I'll have to get an assistant."

By this time he had entered the park. Ahead of him he could hear the running feet of the man he was pursuing. The big recreation ground was almost deserted.

"I don't believe he dare run very fast," reasoned Larry, as he slackened his pace. "If he does a policeman will be sure to stop him and ask questions, and I guess Retto will not relish that. I have a better chance than I thought at first. After all, I don't see why he is so afraid of me. All I want to do is to ask him where he gets the letters from Mr. Potter. He must know where the millionaire is hiding, and it looks as if Mr. Potter had been in Retto's room at the Jackson tenement, or else how would the envelope get there? That's it! I'll bet the missing millionaire has been hiding with this East Indian chap! I never thought of that until now!"

Having walked for fully a quarter of a mile Retto came to a sudden stop, and so did Larry, hiding in the shadow of a tree. Retto listened intently, and, of course, heard no pursuing footsteps. This apparently satisfied him, for he proceeded more slowly.

"He thinks I've given up the chase," thought Larry. "I'll let him. Maybe he'll go home all the quicker, and, after I learn where he is stopping, I can go back and see what Grace wanted."

Larry's surmise proved correct, and his wish soon came to pass. The man, evidently believing that he was safe, emerged from the park to the street, for the whole pursuit had gone on not far from the thoroughfare, and just within the boundary of the city's breathing spot. Larry, keeping in the shadows, watched him.

He saw Retto give one more cautious look around and then, crossing the highway, enter a hotel nearby. It was a fashionable one, and Larry wondered how the man, who had, hitherto, only lived in tenements, could afford to engage rooms in such a place as this.

"Maybe he's only doing it to throw me off the track," the reporter reasoned. "I'll just wait a while and see if he comes out."

He waited nearly an hour, hiding in the shadows of the park and keeping close watch on the entrance to the hotel. He did not see Retto emerge, and then he decided on a new plan.

"I'll inquire if he is stopping there," he said to himself. "If he is I'll wait until to-morrow before acting. I'll let him think everything's all right. It's the best way."

Sauntering into the hotel lobby he found no one but the night clerk on duty, though there were a few sleepy bell-boys sprawled on a bench. As soon as the clerk saw Larry approaching the desk he swung the registry book around, and, dipping a pen in the ink, extended it to the reporter.

"I didn't come to stay," said Larry, with a smile. "I want to inquire if there is a Mr. Mah Retto stopping here?"

"There is," replied the clerk. "Would you like to see him? He just came in a little while ago."

"No; not to-night," Larry replied, his heart beating high with hope. He had run down his man. "I wasn't sure of his address, and I thought I'd inquire. I'll call and see him to-morrow."

The clerk, having lost all interest as soon as he found Larry was not to be a guest of the hotel, did not reply. The bell-boys, seeing their visions of a tip disappearing, resumed their dozes, and Larry walked out. He was impressed by the clerk's manner. Clearly Retto was a man of means and not as poor as Larry had supposed.

"So far so good," he murmured. "Now to go back and see what Grace wanted— that is if it isn't too late."

It was nearly eleven o'clock, but Larry had an idea that Grace would still be up. It was rather an unusual hour to make a call, still all the circumstances in this case were unusual, and Larry did not think Grace would mind.

He saw a light in the Potter house as he approached it. Thinking perhaps Sullivan might be in the vicinity Larry walked up and down on the other side of the street, peering in the shadow of the tree where he had had his encounter with the politician, but Sullivan had evidently gone away.

"Why didn't you come when I called you?" asked Grace, as she admitted Larry to the library.

"I wanted to," the young reporter replied, "but I had to take after a person who I believe knows where your father is, and I couldn't stop without losing sight of him. I have some news for you."

"And I have some for you," exclaimed Grace, "Let me tell mine first."

"All right," agreed Larry, with a smile. "Go ahead."

"Well, I was sitting in the window to-night, looking out on the street, and feeling particularly sad and lonely on account of father, when I saw a man sneaking along on the other side. I saw him hide behind a tree, and I resolved to keep watch. There have been some burglaries in this neighborhood recently, and I wasn't sure whether he was a thief or a detective sent here to watch for suspicious characters. Well, as I sat there watching I saw you come along and talk to the man behind the tree."

"How long had he been there when I came along?"

"Oh, for some time, but don't interrupt, please. You can ask questions afterward. When I saw you talking to the man I knew it must be all right, and I was beginning to think he was a detective.

"Then I noticed another man sneaking along. He, too, hid behind a tree, next to the first man. I thought this was queer until I remembered you told me that detectives usually hunt in couples, and I thought he was another officer from headquarters. I thought so until mother, who, it seems had been looking out of her window in the front room upstairs, called to me.

"She asked me if I had seen the two men come along, and, when I said I had, she wanted to know if I didn't think there was something queer about the second man. I said I didn't notice particularly, but just then the man stepped out into the light, and I had a good look at him."

"Was there anything suspicious about him?"

"There certainly was!" exclaimed Grace, earnestly. "As soon as I saw him I thought sure it was my father. He had his back toward me, and he looked exactly like papa. Mother saw it, too, and she cried out. Just then the man turned and I saw he was smooth-shaven, and his face didn't look a bit like my father's.

"Then I saw you and that other man—Mr. Sullivan, I then knew him to be—step into the light. I saw he was going to hit you, and I raised the window and called. I wanted to ask you to see who the second man was—the one who looked so much like my father. I called, but you didn't seem to hear."

"I heard you," replied Larry, "but I couldn't stop. I wanted to take after the man—the same man you were suspicious of. I traced him through the park."

"Did you find him? Who is he? Where is he? Is he—is he? Oh, Larry, don't keep me in suspense——"

"I'm sorry to have to tell you he isn't your father," Larry replied, gently, as he saw the girl's distress. "But I think he knows where your father is. He goes by the name of Mah Retto, and I helped save him from the wreck of a vessel on the Jersey coast. See, I found this in his room, a little while before he disappeared," and he held out to Grace the torn envelope with her name on it.

"My father's writing!" she exclaimed.

Larry heard some one descending the stairs and coming toward the library.

CHAPTER XXIII

CAPTAIN TANTRELLA ARRIVES

"Grace! What is the matter?" exclaimed a woman's voice, and looking up Larry saw Mrs. Potter.

"Nothing, mother," replied the girl. "This is Mr. Larry Dexter. He just brought me some news. Oh, mother, that wasn't papa we saw out in the street!"

"I knew it, dear, as soon as I saw his face."

Larry felt rather uncomfortable, for Mrs. Potter and Grace showed signs of emotion.

"I was telling your daughter," he said to Mrs. Potter, "that I think I have located the man who knows where your husband is."

"Oh, I hope you have," exclaimed Mrs. Potter. "This suspense is awful. Who is he? Where is he?"

Larry related the circumstances of his chase after Retto, telling how he had located the man at the hotel.

"I'll go and see him to-morrow," he said, "before he has a chance to get away. He does not suspect that I know where he is."

"Why not go now?" asked Mrs. Potter.

"I'm afraid he would see no one to-night. It is very late, and he would suspect something if any one sent up word they wanted to see him. He would at once connect it with the chase I had after him. But I think I fooled him. I am sure he can clear up this matter in a short time, once I get into conversation with him."

"I'll go with you," said Grace, with sudden energy. "I will make him tell where my father is."

Larry thought he could best deal with Retto alone, but he did not want to tell Grace so. However, her mother got him out of what might have been an embarrassing position.

"I'd rather you wouldn't go, Grace," she said. "There is no telling what sort of a person this Retto is. His name sounds foreign."

They talked for some time about the curious circumstances connected with the disappearance of the millionaire, and when a clock struck the hour of one, Larry arose with a start.

"I had no idea it was so late!" he exclaimed. "I must hurry home, or mother will be worried. I will call to-morrow and let you know what success I have."

"Do, please," said Mrs. Potter.

"And come early," added Grace, as she accompanied Larry to the door. "Don't let that horrid man stab you with an East Indian poisoned dagger," she went on with a little laugh, as she got out of hearing of her mother.

Larry promised, and then hurried off down the street to the nearest elevated railway station. He was up early the next morning, and wrote out the story of the day's events, including the encounter with Sullivan, and the chase after Retto. He touched as lightly as possible on his own and Grace's parts in the affair, but there was enough to make interesting reading, and he knew no other paper would have it.

"This is good stuff, Larry," complimented Mr. Emberg, when the reporter had turned his story in at the desk. "What next?"

"I'm going to see Retto," was the answer. "I'll make him tell where Mr. Potter is."

"You were right about your East Indian friend," admitted the city editor. "I had no idea there was a story like this connected with him; least of all that it concerned the missing millionaire. Keep right after him. Let us hear from you in time for the first edition. Whatever you learn from Retto will make the leading part of to-day's account."

"I'll telephone in," said Larry, as he hurried from the city room.

Larry anticipated meeting with some difficulty in getting Retto to talk. He knew the man must have a strong motive for aiding Mr. Potter. Probably the millionaire was paying him well to serve him, to mail letters occasionally, and keep him informed as to how the search for him was progressing.

"There are lots of ends to this that I don't understand," said Larry to himself as he was on his way to the hotel where the mysterious man was stopping. "This mystery seemed to start with the wrecking of the *Olivia*, yet I don't see how I can connect Mr. Potter with that. He must have met Retto in New York after the rescued men came here. Maybe I'm wrong in thinking Mr. Potter is in New York now. He may be some distance off, and depending on Retto to look after his interests. If that's so it would explain why the East Indian was hanging around the house. He wanted to see that Grace and her mother were well, so he could report to the millionaire.

"Yet if that was so, I can't see how Mr. Potter could write in the letter, as he did, that I was getting too close to him? Yes, there's something very strange in all this, but maybe it will soon be cleared up."

Thus Larry hoped, but he was doomed to disappointment. For, when he inquired at the hotel desk for Mr. Retto, and said he would like to see him, the clerk replied:

"Mr. Retto left early this morning. He gave up his room. I don't know where he went."

"I've got it all to do over again," the young reporter thought as he strolled out into the street. "I'll never have such luck again. If he watches the house after this he'll do it in a way that won't give me a chance to catch him. Well, I've got to go back and tell Grace I made a fizzle of it. Too bad, when they're hoping so much on the result of this visit!"

Larry purchased a morning paper from a newsboy on the street, and glanced at it idly, as he strolled along. His eye lighted on the column devoted to shipping news, and, almost unconsciously, he saw among the "arrivals," the *Turtle*, of an Italian line. At once a train of thought was started in his mind.

"The *Turtle*," he mused. "That's the freight ship that Captain Tantrella, formerly of the *Olivia*, commands. That's the captain Retto was inquiring about the day Grace and I made the tour of the steamer offices. He wanted to meet him. Well, Captain Tantrella is in now. I wonder if Retto could have left the hotel to go and see him?"

Larry puzzled over it for a few minutes. Several ideas came to him, but they were confused, and he did not know which line to follow.

"Why should Retto want to see Captain Tantrella?" he asked himself. "Is it possible that Retto is a criminal and had to escape from the sinking ship? It looks so. But if he has done something that would necessitate him keeping out of the way, how can he aid Mr. Potter? It's too deep for me. But I know what

I'll do. I'll go and see Captain Tantrella. He'll remember me, for I interviewed him about the wreck.

"I'll ask him who Retto is. He'll know him, for he was probably one of the first-cabin passengers. That's what I'll do. I think I'm on the right track now."

CHAPTER XXIV

RETTO IS CAUGHT

Larry's slow walk was suddenly changed to a quick one as a plan of action was unfolded in his mind. He hurried to the elevated station and was soon on his way downtown to the office of the steamship line to which the *Turtle* belonged.

"Guess I'd better stop and telephone to Mr. Emberg about Retto skipping out again," thought the young reporter. "He can add it to the story. Then I can tell him of my present plan."

The city editor was soon informed of what Larry intended to do, and said he thought it was a good idea.

"But keep in touch with us, Larry," cautioned Mr. Emberg. "We want all the news we can get on this thing. There's a rumor that the *Scorcher* is going to spring something to-day on the Potter story."

"Probably something Sullivan has given out to offset the story he knows I'll have about him," commented Larry. "But I'll be on the lookout and let you know what happens."

Larry was soon at the steamship office, and inquired whether the *Turtle* had docked yet.

"She is making fast now," replied the clerk.

"May I go aboard her?"

The clerk hesitated. Then Larry announced who he was, and said he wanted to have a talk with Captain Tantrella.

"Oh, you're the reporter who wrote up the wreck of the *Olivia*," the clerk replied, with a smile. "I've heard about you. Yes, I guess you can go aboard. I'll write you out a pass."

With the necessary paper as a passport, Larry walked down the long, covered dock, alongside of which the freight steamer was being warped into place. There was no bustling crowd of passengers, eager to get ashore to welcome and be welcomed by even more eager relatives and friends. But there was a small army of men ready to swarm aboard the *Turtle* and hurry the freight out of her holds, in order that more might be placed in to be sent abroad. There was a confusion of wagons and trucks, and the puffing of donkey engines, seemingly anxious to begin lifting big boxes and bales from the dark interior of the ship.

Larry was among the first to go up the gang plank when it was run ashore. A ship's officer stopped him, but allowed him to proceed when he saw the pass.

Larry found Captain Tantrella in his cabin, arranging his papers, for there is considerable formality about a ship that comes from one country to another, and much red tape is used.

"Ah, it is my newspaper friend!" exclaimed the commander when he saw Larry. "Have you interviewed any more captains who have been wrecked?"

Though he spoke with an air of gayety Larry could see the captain was sad at heart, for, though it was not his fault that the *Olivia* had gone ashore, Captain Tantrella had been more or less blamed, and had been reduced in rank. Passengers do not, as a rule, care to sail in a ship under the command of one whose vessel has been lost. So poor Captain Tantrella was now only in charge of a freighter, and he felt his disgrace keenly.

"Do you remember a passenger named Mah Retto, who sailed with you on the *Olivia*?" the reporter asked.

"I remember him; yes. A queer sort of man. He said but little on the whole voyage. But was he not lost? I remember we could not find him when we had all been landed from the wreck."

"He came ashore first of all," replied Larry. "A fisherman and I helped save him from a life-raft," and he told the circumstances.

"Queer," murmured the captain. "I have often thought of that man. He seemed to have some mystery about him."

Larry gave a brief account of the case he was working on.

"What I want to discover," he added, "is whether you know of any reason why Retto should be anxious to see you?"

"To see me?"

"Yes. He was at the steamship office a few days ago inquiring when your ship would come in, and when he saw me he hurried away. Since then I have not been able to catch him."

"Ah! I know!" exclaimed the captain suddenly. "I just thought of it. I have a package belonging to him."

"A package?"

"Yes. He came to me when we were a few days out and said he wanted me to keep a package for him until we got to New York. I took it and put it with my papers."

"Then I suppose it was lost with the *Olivia*?"

"No; I brought it ashore with me when I saved my documents and a few valuables from the wreck. I have it at my hotel. That is why he is anxious to see me. He wants to get his package back. I am glad I have it."

"Do you know anything about the man?" asked Larry.

"Hardly anything. I met him for the first time when he was a passenger on my ship. But now, if you have no objections, we will go ashore. I must file my reports. After that I will be glad to see you at my hotel, and answer any questions you care to ask."

"Well, I guess you've told me all you can," said Larry, feeling a little disappointed at the result of his interview. "I'm much obliged to you."

"If you want to get into communication with this man, I have a plan," suggested the captain.

"What?" asked Larry, eagerly.

"He will probably call at my hotel to claim his package. When he comes you could be on hand."

"But there is no telling when he will come."

"That is so, but you could take a room at the hotel and be there as much as possible. I think he will come as soon as he learns that my ship is in."

"That's a good idea. I'll do it!" exclaimed Larry.

"Then let's hurry ashore, and you can make your arrangements while I finish up the details of the indents, bills of lading, custom lists and so on," Captain Tantrella said.

The two walked down the gang plank on to the covered dock. The tangle of wagons, horses and men was worse than ever. Part of the cargo was being taken out and carted away.

"Watch out for yourself that a horse doesn't step on you," cautioned the captain.

It was a needful warning, for the animals, drawing big, heavy trucks, seemed to be every-where. As the two proceeded to thread their way through the maze there came a hail from somewhere in the rear and a voice called:

"Captain Tantrella!"

The commander turned, and so did Larry. The young reporter saw a man hurrying along the dock toward where the commander of the *Turtle* stood. Evidently he had not seen the captain come to a halt, for he called again:

"Wait a minute, Captain Tantrella!"

Then a curious thing happened. The man caught sight of Larry, standing beside the ship commander. He halted and turned to run. As he did so a truck drove up behind him and blocked his retreat.

"It's Mah Retto!" exclaimed Larry, as he caught sight of the man's face.

An instant later there came a warning shout from the driver of the truck. He reined his horses back sharply, but not in time. Retto had stepped directly under their heads. The off animal reared. The man stumbled and fell beneath its hoofs.

Then, with a cry of terror, which was echoed by a score of men who saw the accident, Retto appeared to crumple up in a heap. The forefeet of the big steed seemed to crush him before the driver could back the animal off. Then came silence, Retto lying without moving on the planking of the dock.

"Caught at last," murmured Larry, as he rushed forward.

CHAPTER XXV

IN THE HOSPITAL

Instantly the confusion that had reigned on the dock became worse. Men ran to and fro shouting, no one seeming to know what to do.

"We must help him!" cried Captain Tantrella, shoving his papers into his pocket. "Come!"

He and Larry fought their way to the man's side. A crowd surrounded him, but no one offered to do anything. The truck driver had dismounted from his high seat and was quieting his frightened horses.

"It wasn't my fault," he cried. "He ran right under their feet."

"One side!" exclaimed a loud voice, and a burly policeman shouldered his way through. "What's the matter? Give the man some air."

Retto did not look as though he would ever need air again. He seemed quite dead.

"Let me get at him!" called Captain Tantrella. "I know something of medicine."

"Shall I call an ambulance?" asked Larry of the police officer. "I know how to do it."

The bluecoat nodded, glad to have help in the emergency. Then he proceeded to keep the crowd back while the captain knelt down beside the unfortunate man.

"Bad cut on the head," the commander of the *Turtle* murmured. "Fractured, I'm afraid. Leg broken, too. It's a wonder he wasn't killed."

The captain accepted several coats which were hastily offered, and made a pillow for the man's head. He arranged the broken leg so that the bones would be in a better position for setting, and then, with a sponge and a basin of water which were brought, proceeded to wipe away the blood from the cut on Retto's skull.

The crowd increased and pressed closer, but by this time more policemen had arrived, and they kept the throng back from the sufferer, so that he might have air.

It seemed a long time before the ambulance, which Larry summoned, made its arrival, but it was only a few minutes ere it clanged up to the pier, the crowd parting to let it pass. In an instant the white-suited surgeon had leaped out of the back of the vehicle before it had stopped, and was kneeling beside Retto.

With deft fingers he felt of the wound on the man's head.

"Possible fracture," he said in a low voice. "Double one of the leg, I'm afraid," as he glanced at that member. "Lend a hand, boys, and we'll get him on the stretcher."

There were willing enough helpers, and Retto was soon in the ambulance and on the way to the hospital, the doctor clinging to the back of the swaying vehicle as it dashed through the streets, with the right of way over everything on wheels.

"Here's news in bunches," thought Larry, as he saw the ambulance disappearing around a corner. "I must telephone this in, and I guess it will be a beat. To think that after all that I have Retto where I want him. I'm sorry, of course, that he's hurt, but I guess he can't get out of the hospital very soon. I'll have a chance to question him. Then I'll make him tell me where Mr. Potter is, and that will end my special assignment. I'll not be sorry, either. It's been a hard one, though I'm glad I got it, for the experience is fine."

Thus musing Larry looked for a telephone station and soon the story of Retto's accident was being sent over the wire to the city editor.

"This will make a fine lead for our Potter story," said Larry, as he finished telling of the accident.

"I've got another plan," said Mr. Emberg.

"What is it?"

"Do you think anyone else knows who Retto is? I mean anyone on the pier who saw him hurt?"

"I think not. Captain Tantrella might, but other reporters are not likely to connect him with the case."

"Then this is what I'm going to do. I'll use the story of the accident separate from the Potter story. We'll say an unidentified man was run down on the pier.

If he has a fractured skull he'll not be able to tell who he is, and he has probably taken good care that there are no papers in his clothes by which his name can be learned.

"If we state that the injured man is the mysterious Retto, who is mixed up in the Potter case, we'll have every reporter in New York camping out at that hospital waiting for a chance to get the information from him. If we keep quiet we may be able to get it ourselves without any of the others knowing it. We'll try that way, Larry. It's a risk, but you've got to take risks in this business."

The young reporter admired the generalship of his city editor, who could thus plan a magnificent beat. Larry saw the feasibility of the plan. If he kept his information to himself no one would know but what the injured man was a stranger in New York, and that he was connected with the Potter case would be farthest from the thoughts of any reporters who were working on the missing millionaire story.

"You must camp on his trail, Larry," Mr. Emberg went on. "As soon as you hear from the hospital people that he is in shape to talk, get in to see him. You can truthfully claim to be a friend and acquaintance, for you once helped to save his life. If you get a chance to talk to him, ask where Potter is, and let us know at once. We'll get out an extra, if need be. Now hurry over to the hospital and let us hear from you as soon as possible. Get a good story and a beat."

"I only hope I can," murmured Larry, as he left the telephone booth and started for the hospital to which Retto had been taken.

He had a slight acquaintance with the superintendent of the institution, and when he explained his errand the official agreed to let Larry in to see the man as soon as the nurses and surgeons had finished dressing his injuries.

"How is he?" asked Larry.

The superintendent called over a private telephone connected with the ward where Retto had been taken:

"How is the patient just brought in from the pier? Comfortable, eh? That's good."

Then he turned to Larry:

"I guess you can go up soon," he added. "Can you give us his name, and some particulars? He was unconscious when he came in," and the superintendent prepared to jot down the information on his record book.

This was a complication Larry had not foreseen. If he gave the superintendent the fugitive's name, any other reporters who came to the hospital to inquire about the injured man would at once connect Retto with the Potter mystery, and the *Leader's* chance for a beat would be small indeed. What was he to do? He decided to take the superintendent partly into his confidence.

"I know the name he goes by," he said, as the beginning of his account, "but I do not believe it is his right one. I think it is an alias he uses."

"Never mind then," the superintendent interrupted, much to Larry's relief. "If it's a false name we don't want it."

"I believe it is," Larry added, and he was honest in that statement, for he felt that Retto was playing some deep game, and, in that case, would not be likely to use his right name.

"We don't want our records wrong," the head of the hospital resumed. "We'll wait until he can tell us about himself."

The telephone bell rang at that juncture, and the superintendent answering it told Larry the patient was now in bed and could be seen.

"Don't get him excited," cautioned the official. "I want to get some information from him about himself when you are through."

It is sometimes the custom in New York, in accident cases, to allow reporters to interview the victims, when their physical condition admits of it. So it was no new thing for Larry to go into the hospital ward to speak to Retto. He passed through rows of white cots, on which reclined men in all stages of disease and accident. There was a sickish smell of iodoform in the atmosphere, and the sight of the pale faces on either side made Larry sad at heart.

"There's your patient," said a nurse who was with him, as she led Larry to the bed where Retto reclined under the white coverings that matched the hue of his face. "Now don't excite him. You newspaper men don't care what you do as long as you get a story, and sometimes all the work we nurses do goes for nothing."

"I'll be careful," promised Larry.

The nurse, who had other duties to keep her busy, left Larry at the bedside of the mysterious man. He was lying with his eyes shut as Larry approached.

"Mr. Retto," called the reporter.

There was no response.

"Mr. Retto," spoke Larry, a little louder.

At that the man opened his eyes.

"Were you calling me?" he asked. Then he caught sight of Larry, and a smile came on his face.

"Well, you've found me, I see," was his greeting. "Only for that team I'd been far away."

"I suppose so. But now you're here, for which I'm sorry; I hope you will answer me a few questions."

"What are they?" asked the man, and a spasm of pain replaced his smile.

"I believe you know the secret of Mr. Potter's disappearance," said Larry, speaking in a low tone so none of the other patients would hear him. "I want you to tell me where he is."

At the mention of Mr. Potter's name Retto raised himself in bed. His face that had been pale became flushed.

"He—he—is——" then he stopped. He seemed unable to speak.

"Yes—yes!" exclaimed Larry, eagerly. "Where is he?"

"He—is——"

Then Retto fell back on the bed.

"He has fainted!" cried the nurse, running to the cot. "The strain has been too much for him," and she pressed an electric button which summoned the doctor.

CHAPTER XXVI

A NEW CLUE

Larry moved to one side. The unexpected outcome of his interview had startled him. He did not quite know what to do.

The doctor came up on the run and made a hasty examination of the patient. Then he sent for another surgeon. Larry heard them talking.

"What is it?" he asked of his friend the nurse.

"His skull is fractured," she said in a low voice. "They did not think so at first, but now the symptoms show it. They are going to operate at once. It is the only chance of saving his life."

"There goes my story," thought Larry, regretfully.

It was not that he was hard-hearted or indifferent to Retto's sufferings. Simply that his newspaper instinct got ahead of everything else, as it does in all true reporters, who, if they have a "nose for news," will make "copy" out of even their closest friend, though they may dislike the operation very much.

"You had better go," the nurse advised Larry. "You will not be able to see him again for some time—no one will be allowed to talk to him until he is on the road to recovery—if we can save him. He has a bad fracture."

Much disappointed, Larry left the hospital. It was hard to be almost on the verge of getting the story and then to see his chance slip away.

"I'm sure he was just going to tell me where Mr. Potter is," thought the reporter. "Now it means a long wait, if I ever find out at all from him."

He told Mr. Emberg what had happened. The city editor decided to follow out his first plan, of not connecting the accident at the pier with the Potter mystery.

"If he has to be operated on for a fractured skull," Mr. Emberg remarked to Larry over the wire, "he will be in no condition to tell his name, or give any information for some time. The story is safe with him. Now you'd better get busy on some other line of the case. The *Scorcher* is out, but they only have a scare yarn, without any foundation, to the effect that Mr. Potter is still in Italy, and that his family knows where he is."

"That's all bosh!" exclaimed Larry.

"That's what I think," the city editor said. "Now get on the job, Larry, and arrange to give us a good story for to-morrow. Keep watch of Retto, and as soon as the doctors will let you see him try again, though of course it may not be for several days."

Larry was all at sea. He hung up the telephone receiver with a vague feeling that being a reporter on a special assignment was not all it was cracked up to be.

"Easy enough to say get a good story for to-morrow," he remarked to himself, "but I'd like to know how I'm going to do it? The story—the only story there is—is safe with Retto, and he can't tell it."

"What shall I do?" Larry asked himself. "Let me think. I guess I'd better go see Captain Tantrella and ask him to keep mum about Retto until I have another chance at the man. Then I'll—I'll go and tell Grace. She'll want to know all about it."

He found Captain Tantrella at his hotel, having finished all the details connected with the docking of the *Turtle*. The commander readily agreed to keep quiet concerning Retto's identity, since the captain had no desire for further newspaper notoriety.

"I will do more than this," he declared. "I will give you the package belonging to that queer man. I have to sail again soon, on a long voyage, and he might need it before I come back. You can give it to him if he recovers. If he does not—well, the authorities can open it. It may contain money or something that will tell about the poor fellow. I leave it with you."

Larry was glad to get possession of the package that seemed of such importance to Retto. He wished he could open it, as he thought he might get a clue to the connection between the millionaire and the mysterious man, but he knew he would have no right to do that. Also it would give him a sort of claim on Retto, and, by returning the package, he could have a good excuse for going to see him.

"Now to tell Grace," remarked Larry, as he left Captain Tantrella. "I'm sure she'll be anxious to hear the news."

The millionaire's daughter was indeed glad to see Larry. She had read the first edition of the *Leader*, and wanted to know if there was anything further to tell.

"I hoped to be able to give you some definite news," replied Larry, in answer to her questions. Then he related the scene in the hospital.

"Poor man!" exclaimed Grace. "I wish I could go and see him."

"I'm afraid they wouldn't let you," said the reporter. "I called up the place just before I came here and they said the man was still under the influence of ether, though the operation was over."

"Was it a success?"

"They think so, but it will be some time before he will be able to talk to anyone about your father. We shall have to be patient."

"It is so hard," complained Grace, and Larry agreed with her. He did not yet see how he was going to get a story for the next day's paper—that is, a story which would have some fresh features in it.

"I don't suppose you have anything new to tell me?" he asked of Grace.

"Not much. I have had another letter from my father. It came a little while ago."

"Is it the same as the others?"

"The contents are, but the envelope is different. He says he will soon be home, and tells us not to worry."

She gave the missive to Larry. He looked at the post-mark, and saw that it had come from a downtown sub-station.

"This was mailed near the steamer pier!" he exclaimed. "Close to where Retto was hurt. He must have posted it just previous to the accident. I wish I had known this before."

It was too late now, and Larry gazed regretfully at the envelope. Clearly, Retto had not been far from Mr. Potter at the time of the accident. Perhaps the missing millionaire was hiding downtown in New York.

"I must make some inquiries in that neighborhood," thought Larry, as he arose to go.

"Another thing," Grace said. "That man Sullivan was in front of the house again this morning."

"I must see him!" exclaimed Larry. "I'll make him tell what his object is. This thing has got to end!"

He was fiercely determined that he would force some information from the politician. Evidently Sullivan had a game on hand which the reporter had not yet succeeded in fathoming. "I'll hunt him up at once!" he added, as he bade Grace good-bye.

"Be careful," she cautioned. "He is a dangerous man."

"I will," Larry promised.

But he could not find Sullivan. For once that wily politician denied himself to reporters, and kept out of their way. He was sought by a number of newspaper men, for the matter of a candidate for the eighth assembly district was again to the fore, and the henchmen of Kilburn and Reilly were making rival claims as to Sullivan's support.

"Where is Sullivan?" was the cry that went up, and in the next two days that became almost as much of a mystery as the disappearance of Mr. Potter.

"Get busy, Larry," advised Mr. Emberg, and Larry did his best to follow the advice.

Three weeks passed, and Sullivan was not found. His family professed not to know where he was, and the best newspaper men in New York could not find him. Larry was working on the case with all the energy he had thrown into the Potter disappearance.

Meanwhile the young reporter kept a close watch on the hospital where Retto was. The operation had been a success, but the patient was in a fever, during which he was out of his mind. He could not recognize anyone, much less talk intelligibly. Larry made several calls at the institution, but it was of no use.

"You can't see him," said the nurse, when he had paid his usual visit one day, "but he is much better. I think by the day after to-morrow you can talk to him. His fever is going down and he has spells when he talks rationally. There was another man in to see him to-day."

"I thought you said no one could visit him."

"Well, we made an exception in this case. The man was a private detective, searching for a missing man, and he wanted to see all the patients. He looked at your friend last, and went off, seemingly quite excited."

"What missing man was he looking for?" asked Larry.

"A Mr. Potter. Seems to me I've read something about him in the papers. He's very rich."

"Mr. Potter!" exclaimed Larry. "The detective must be from the private agency," he added to himself. Then aloud: "Did he recognize Mr. Ret—er I mean the man with the fractured skull?" and he waited anxiously for the nurse's answer.

"He seemed to, but I was called away just then."

"I know how Mr. Potter looks," Larry went on. "He has a moustache, and the man here is smooth-shaven."

"No, the patient has a moustache and a beard now," the nurse replied with a smile. "They grew since he has been in the hospital."

A sudden idea came to Larry. An idea so strange that it startled him. He dared not speak of it. He believed the detective held the same theory.

"I'll call again," he said, thanking the nurse for the information she had given him. "I must see Grace at once," he murmured, as he left the hospital. "Strange I never thought of that. A beard and a moustache! The private detective! I wonder if he recognized Retto? I must hurry. Oh, if this should prove true!"

He hurried to an elevated station and was soon on his way to Grace's house.

CHAPTER XXVII

THE DETECTIVE'S THEORY

Bounding up the steps three at a time Larry rang the bell of the Potter residence. He thought the door would never be opened, and, when the stately butler did swing back the portal the young reporter, not waiting to ask for anyone, stepped into the hall.

"No one at home," the servant remarked with a smile, for he had gotten to be on quite friendly terms with Larry.

"No one home?"

"No. Mrs. Potter and Miss Grace have gone to Lakewood, N.J., for a few days. Mrs. Potter was quite ill, and the doctor advised a change of air, so she suddenly decided to go."

"When are they coming back?"

"I can't rightly say. In a few days, I expect. I was told to tell you that if anything important occurred you could write to them. Here is the address," and the butler gave Larry a slip of paper.

"I wonder whether I ought to telegraph?" thought Larry to himself. "I think this is very important, yet I am not sure enough of it myself. I can't see Retto until the day after to-morrow. I had better wait until then. If my suspicions are confirmed I will send a message, in case they are not back by that time."

Larry was about to leave the house when he saw a man coming up the front steps. He recognized him as a member of the private detective agency which he and Grace had visited.

"Is Mrs. Potter home?" asked the man of the butler, who was standing in the opened front door, while Larry remained in the shadow of the hall.

"No, she has gone to Lakewood."

"Lakewood! That's too bad!" exclaimed the man.

"Is it anything important?" inquired the butler.

"I think I have located Mr. Potter," was the answer. "I am a private detective, hired by Miss Grace Potter. I came to see if she or her mother would accompany me to try to identify a man I believe is the missing millionaire."

"Where is he?" asked the butler.

"In a hospital, quite badly hurt."

"Mr. Potter in a hospital! Badly hurt!" cried the servant in alarm. "What shall I do? Can't they bring him home?"

"We must be sure it is him," the detective went on. "The description answers pretty well, but it would take a member of the family to make sure. So there's no one home, eh? Well, that's toobad. I wanted to test my theory that the hospital patient is the missing millionaire."

"You can telegraph to them," suggested the butler. "I have the address."

"That's what I'll do," the detective replied. "I'll tell them what I have discovered. They can get here to-morrow and we'll see if he's the right man."

The officer took the address the servant gave him and hurried away.

"Did you hear that?" cried the butler to Larry. "Mr. Potter is found!"

"I hope it proves true," the reporter replied. "That is just what I came about, but when I found Mrs. Potter gone I didn't know what to do. I had rather the detective would take the responsibility of telegraphing. Perhaps the man in the hospital is not Mr. Potter?"

"Do you know him?" asked the butler.

"I have met him several times," replied Larry, "but I did not know he was Mr. Potter. It just dawned on me that he might be."

"Well, well, how strange it all is," murmured the butler. "Who would have thought it? Well, we can't do anything until to-morrow."

"No, I guess not," answered Larry, as he went down the steps.

His mind was in a tumult. More and more he was coming to believe that the mysterious man in the hospital was the missing millionaire.

"That's what he meant when he said I was following him too close," mused Larry. "And I never suspected it! How glad Grace will be! What a story I shall have! I wish I had discovered him myself, without any help from the detective agency, but it will make good reading, anyhow. I must arrange it so we can get a scoop out of it."

His first act was to go to the office of the paper and tell Mr. Emberg what had occurred. The city editor was much excited by the news.

"That will make a great yarn!" he exclaimed. "I hope your friend Grace soon comes back with her mother and makes the identification complete. We must do nothing to hasten matters or some other paper will get on to the game and spoil our story."

"Even the hospital people don't suspect yet," said Larry. "They don't know who their patient is—not even his assumed name."

"I guess things are coming our way. We'll clear up the Potter mystery and the Sullivan disappearance at the same time. I believe Sullivan is in with Mr. Potter on some deal. It begins to look suspicious. The friends of Reilly and Kilburn are all at sea. They'd give a thousand dollars to know which way Sullivan was going to jump."

Larry paid an early visit to the hospital the next day to see how matters were progressing. His friend, the nurse, greeted him with a smile.

"I guess you can have an interview with your mysterious acquaintance now," she said. "He is much better than we expected, and, for the first time since the operation, talks rationally. We have not questioned him yet. We are not as curious as you newspaper men are."

"Well, we have to be," responded Larry. "Can I go up now? Has the man who was here yesterday been back?"

"Yes to your first question, and no to the second. You can go up. The superintendent left word to that effect. He is quite friendly to you."

Larry started for the ward where Retto was. His heart was beating strangely. He felt that he was on the verge of solving the secret of the millionaire's disappearance and restoring to Grace her father.

As he approached the bed where Retto reclined he was motioned back by another nurse on duty there.

"He has just fallen asleep," she said. "When he awakens again you may speak to him. He has been writing a letter."

Larry was disappointed. He looked at the man who had played such an important part in the disappearance of the millionaire, and who, he believed, was destined to assume a much more important rôle. The patient's beard and moustache had grown since the accident, and the smooth-shaven man was no more. Instead, Larry saw before him a person who, as he recalled thephotographs of Mr. Potter, bore a remarkable resemblance to the millionaire.

Of course, Mr. Potter had only a moustache and no beard, but aside from that Larry was positive that, lying on the bed in front of him, was Grace's father.

CHAPTER XXVIII

A TERRIBLE MISTAKE

How Larry wished the patient would awaken so he could question him! But the invalid showed no signs of it, and was in a deep slumber.

"That will do him more good than medicine," said the nurse. "He will probably sleep for several hours."

"Several hours," repeated Larry in dismay.

"Yes, they often do."

"Then there is no use in me waiting," he said. "I'll come back again. When I do I may bring his daughter with me."

"I hope you do," the nurse replied. "I have felt so sorry for the poor man. He seemed to have no friends ever since he has been here. Who is he?"

"I don't want to say for sure, until I get his daughter to identify him," Larry said, for he did not want the story to get out before the *Leader* had a chance to print it.

He decided he would go to the Potter house and see if Grace had returned yet in response to the telegram sent by the detective. He felt sure she would start immediately on receipt of the message.

In this he was correct, for when he got to the millionaire's home Grace herself answered his ring.

"Oh, Larry! Tell me quick!" she exclaimed. "Where is he? Is he badly hurt? What is the matter? Do you think it is really he?"

"I hope so," Larry said. "Where is your mother?"

"She stayed in Lakewood. I didn't tell her anything about it, for fear it would prove a disappointment. The telegram from the detective came to me and I made up my mind to come home alone and clear matters up before I told mother. She needs a rest, as she is very nervous.

"But now I am here, you must take me to the hospital at once. The telegram said he was in a hospital. How did it happen? Is he badly hurt?"

"I think he is almost well."

"But how did they discover him? Who did it? How did it come about?"

"It will take some time to answer all the questions," replied Larry with a smile. "I'll tell you all I can on the way to the hospital. My mysterious friend, Mah Retto, it seems, has turned out to be your father."

"Then he was the one I saw in front of the house that night, and I thought it was father," said Grace. "His smooth-shaven face deceived me, but I was sure I could not mistake his figure."

"There have been a good many surprises in this case," Larry admitted. "I've often been fooled myself."

"Let's hurry to the hospital," suggested Grace. "I'd rather go with you than with that detective. He is to be here at eleven o'clock, and it's only ten now. Let's hurry away."

Larry agreed, and they left the house. Grace explained that she had caught the first express out of Lakewood that morning and had been home only half an hour when Larry called.

They were so busy talking over all the details of the queer case that they arrived at the hospital much quicker than they anticipated.

"Here we are," said Larry, as he led the way up the broad stone steps of the institution.

"I'm almost afraid to go in," remarked Grace, her voice showing a nervous dread. "It seems so strange. I'm quite frightened, Larry."

"Don't think of anything but that you're going to see your father," the reporter replied, reassuringly. "He'll be so glad to see you. I believe he would have been home long before this if it had not been for the accident."

Larry entered the office of the institution. No sooner had he stepped inside than he was made aware that something unusual had occurred. Nurses and doctors, with anxious looks, were hastening here and there. Orderlies and messengers were hurrying to and fro, and there was a continuous ringing of signal and telephone bells.

"Must have been an accident and a lot of patients bought in," said Larry, for he had seen such activity in hospitals before when a number of injured persons required treatment at once.

"Oh, how terrible!" exclaimed Grace. "Do you suppose many are killed?"

"I hope not. But it looks as if something very unusual had happened."

Just then Larry saw the nurse who had been at the bedside of the patient whom he and Grace had come to see.

"I've brought his daughter," he said to the uniformed attendant. "May we go up now?"

The nurse seemed confused.

"I don't know—I'll see!" she remarked. "Here is the superintendent. Perhaps you had better speak to him," and she whispered something to the official.

"There's something wrong about Mr. Potter!" was Larry's first thought. "I wonder if he could have suddenly died?"

Even Grace, unaccustomed as she was to hospital scenes, was aware that all was not as it should be.

"Oh, Larry!" she exclaimed. "What is the matter? Have they taken him away?"

"I don't know," the reporter answered in a low tone. "I'll soon find out."

The superintendent approached them.

"You wanted to see that patient who was brought in from the steamship pier?" he inquired. "We've never been able to obtain his name."

"I can tell you what it is," answered Larry. "We have every reason to believe he is Hamden Potter, the missing millionaire, and this young lady's father. May we see him?"

"Hamden Potter!" exclaimed the superintendent.

"That's who he is," declared Larry. "He went by the name Mah Retto while he was away. May we go up now?"

"I am sorry," said the superintendent slowly, "but that patient escaped from the ward about half an hour ago, and we have not been able to trace him!"

"Escaped!" cried Larry.

"My father gone again!" gasped Grace.

"Too bad, but that's what has happened," the superintendent repeated. "The nurse left him sleeping quietly, and went downstairs to get some medicine. When she came back he was gone."

"But how could he go out without any clothing?" asked Larry.

"He got some clothing," the head of the institution replied. "In the bed next to him was a patient who was to be discharged as cured to-day. That man's clothes were brought to him and laid out on a chair beside the bed. While he was in the bathroom Mr. Potter, as you call him, got possession of the clothes, put them on, and walked out. Several patients saw him go, but said nothing, as they thought it was all right. When the nurse got back she missed your friend and gave the alarm."

"Can't you tell in what direction he went?" asked Larry.

"So far we have been unsuccessful. We have made inquiries outside, but so many persons are passing in the street that it has been impossible to trace him."

"Was he able to walk very far?" the reporter asked.

"He was strong; much stronger than the usual run of patients who are recovering from such a wound as he had. He must have been more fully recovered than we thought. He had written a letter, the nurse tells me, and this is also gone. Probably he was temporarily out of his mind, and went out to mail the missive. It is a strange occurrence."

"My poor father!" exclaimed Grace. "I thought I had found him, and now he is missing again."

Larry did not know what to do. It was a curious state of affairs. He had been so sure of uniting Mr. Potter and Grace, but now all his plans had come to nothing. Then, too, there was the paper to be considered. Mr. Emberg would expect him to send in the story of the mysterious disappearance of the hospital patient. Yet

Larry did not like to leave Grace while he went to telephone. He was in a curious predicament.

"We will send out a general alarm if we do not find him soon," the superintendent went on. "Occasionally delirious patients wander from the wards while the nurses are temporarily absent, but they are always found hiding in some part of the hospital. We have not yet completed the search. Only once in a great while do they get outside the institution. Yet Mr. Potter may have."

"Then we may never find him again," spoke Grace.

"Don't worry," Larry advised, as cheerfully as he could. "He'll come back."

"I'll never see him again!" and Grace was on the verge of tears. "Oh, this is terrible!"

Just then there was heard a confusion of sounds in the corridor outside of the superintendent's office. The latter went to the door, and through the opened portal Grace and Larry heard some one exclaim:

"He's come back!"

"Maybe that's him!" cried the reporter.

The superintendent returned to his office.

"I have a pleasant surprise for you," he exclaimed. "The patient has come back. He says he went out to a telephone."

"Is he—is he all right?" asked Grace.

"Better than ever. The little trip seemed to do him good. Here he is."

He threw open the door he had closed. There, standing in the corridor, was the man Larry had known as Mah Retto—the man he believed was Mr. Potter. The patient was smiling at the reporter.

"There is your father, Grace," said Larry.

The girl gave one look at the man confronting her. She seemed to sway forward, and became deathly pale——

"That is not my father!" she cried, as she fell in a faint.

CHAPTER XXIX

IN HIS ENEMIES' POWER

"Quick! Catch her!" cried the hospital superintendent, springing forward, but it was Larry who put out his arms and kept Grace from falling to the floor.

"Here, nurse," called one of several physicians who had gathered in the corridor when the news spread that the missing patient had returned. "Look after her, please. Carry her into the receiving room."

"Who is she?" asked the patient, who had caused such a stir, and to whom no one seemed to be paying any attention in the excitement caused by Grace's swoon. The man had not caught a good look at the girl.

"She is Grace Potter," replied Larry, glancing curiously at Mah Retto.

"Grace Potter? Hamden Potter's daughter?" The man seemed greatly excited.

"Yes. She came here expecting, as I did, to meet her father. I thought you were Mr. Potter. She says you are not."

"No, I am not," replied the man.

"Then who are you? Where is her father? You know! I am sure of it!" Larry was upset over the mistake he and the detective had made.

"I did know where Mr. Potter was," and as he made that answer Retto gave every evidence of being under a great strain. His hands shook with more than the weakness of his illness. He was paler than the white hue caused by his confinement in the hospital.

"Why? Have you lost track of him?"

"I am afraid so. Listen, young man, perhaps you can help me. Let us get to some place where we can talk. I have strange news for you."

"Then you know me?" and the young reporter looked somewhat surprised.

"I couldn't very well help it, with the way you have kept after me lately. But we have no time to lose. Something most unexpected has happened. Mr. Potter is in the hands of his enemies!"

"Then he is found?"

"Yes, in a way, but he might better be lost!"

"What do you mean?"

"Come in here and I will tell you."

Retto led the way to a small room off the main corridor.

"What does this mean?" asked the hospital superintendent.

"I will explain later," replied Retto. "Just now it is very necessary that I have a talk with this young man."

The superintendent turned away and Retto closed the door. He sat down in a chair, and Larry could see that he was trembling from weakness.

"I must talk quickly," he said, "for I am still very ill. I made a desperate effort to go out in order to get in communication with Mr. Potter. I mailed him a letter and then called him up on the telephone——"

"Then you know where he was!" burst out Larry.

"I did, but I do not now. Listen, and don't ask too many questions yet. All will soon be explained, if it is not too late. I am Mr. Potter's friend. He took me into his confidence when he found it necessary, for very strong reasons, to disappear. I agreed to help him and do exactly as he wanted me to. He has been hiding across the Hudson River, outside of the legal jurisdiction of New York State. I was in touch with him by telephone and otherwise up to the time of my accident on the pier. Since then, of course, I have not been able to hold any communication with him. As soon as I had the chance, which came for the first time to-day, I got out and called him on the telephone. I was told by the man, with whom he had been staying, that, about an hour ago, some men came and took him away."

"Some men took him away?"

"Yes. Men whom I recognized, by the description, as his enemies—as men who have an interest in getting Mr. Potter into their power. He has been trying all this while to keep out of their way. Now they have him!"

"But what's to be done?" asked the young reporter.

"I don't know," replied Retto, hopelessly. "Everything was going on all right until those horses knocked me down."

Larry was conscious of a strange sensation. It was partly due to his impetuosity he felt that Retto had been injured. Larry partly blamed himself for Mr. Potter's present plight, since through the reporter's instrumentality the millionaire's friend had not been able to keep in touch with him.

"I'll find him!" exclaimed Larry. "Tell me what to do! I'll trace him!"

"If I was only stronger!" said Retto. "I'm so weak that I couldn't walk another block. I'd like to get after those scoundrels who have Mr. Potter!"

"I'll get after them!" cried the youthful newspaper man, thinking more of Grace just then than he did of his assignment. "Tell me where to go!"

"I can only tell you where Mr. Potter was hiding," went on Retto. "That was in a little house just outside of Jersey City. The men must have gone there after him. Possibly you can trace them from the house."

"Tell me how to get to the place!"

Retto gave the necessary instructions.

"I'm going over there!" exclaimed the young reporter.

"What are you going to do with Grace?"

"That's so! I forgot about her. I'll take her along!" and Larry sprang to his feet in his enthusiasm and started for the door.

"Can she stand the trip?"

"She's a brave girl! She'll be glad to go!"

"Then you'd better hurry. Every minute is precious. Great things hang on this. If Mr. Potter's enemies force him to do certain things, which he has been trying to avoid doing, the consequences will be very bad for many persons. Hurry, Dexter!"

"I'll start at once. I wonder if Grace is better?"

The young reporter and Retto left the small room. Larry soon found that Grace had recovered from her swoon. Rapidly he told her of what he proposed doing. With her he would go to Jersey City and try to trace the missing millionaire.

"And we'll find him!" he added, with vigor.

He went downstairs to telephone to Mr. Emberg of the new and unexpected turn the case had taken.

"Keep right after it, Larry!" said the city editor. "Find Mr. Potter and get the story!"

As the *Leader* reporter turned to go upstairs he saw, entering the hospital, a young man whom he recognized as Hans Fritsch, the German newspaper man he had met at the lonely tenement.

"What are you doing here?" asked Larry, noting that his friend was attired in an automobile suit.

"I comes to see how gets along a friend of mine. He is here sick. I have a day off from mine work and I comes in my new automobile. After dot I goes me for a nice ride. Come along!"

"Where are you going?" asked Larry, a sudden idea coming into his head.

"Ofer by New Jersey. Dere is goot automobiling roads."

"Are you going to Jersey City?"

"Sure. I goes by dot on der ferry. Den I skips out by der Plank Roat, und maybe I goes me out to der Oranges Mountains. I am just learning to run my car goot!"

"I'll go with you!" cried Larry. "Have you room in your car for two?"

"Surely! For four, if you likes to bring 'em. My mother, who is in Germany, und quite vell off, send me der car for a birthday present, odervise I should not haff him. Reporters here do not get monies enough to buy automobiles!"

"I'll be with you in five minutes!" exclaimed Larry, hurrying off to tell Grace.

"I am ready as soon as I see how my sick friend is," declared the German reporter. "Den we go quick like de wind, und haff a goot time!"

"Yes, and maybe a hot pursuit!" said Larry under his breath, for he had determined on a bold plan. He would, in Fritsch's auto, give chase to the captors of Mr. Potter.

CHAPTER XXX

MR. POTTER IS FOUND—CONCLUSION

There was a throbbing of the motor, a grinding and shrieking as the clutch was thrown in, a trembling to the car as Fritsch advanced the spark and opened the gasolene throttle still wider and the automobile, bearing the German reporter, Larry and Grace, was off.

"Here are some goggles!" said Fritsch, handing back two pairs to his passengers. "You vill need dem when ve goes like de wind. If I had known I was to haff a lady I would get a dust coat."

"It doesn't matter," replied Grace, her eyes shining with the excitement. "I want to find my father."

"Your father?"

Then Larry explained. He could safely do so since the German paper did not come out until the morning of the next day, and Fritsch could not "beat" him.

Faster speeded the auto. They went over the Hudson River on a ferry boat, and, as soon as Jersey City was reached, the car was sent along as fast as the law allowed.

"I wonder if I can get on their trail?" thought Larry, as he watched the houses skim by, and held himself in his seat, beside Grace, to avoid the jouncing and swaying caused by the uneven streets.

"Do you think ve vill haff a race?" asked the German, as they neared the house where Mr. Potter had been hiding.

"Maybe. I hope so, anyhow."

"I don't."

"Why? Don't you want to help find Mr. Potter?"

"Yes, but I am of nervousness yet in my new car. I haff never raced, und I might do some damage."

"Let me run her," suggested Larry. "I've had some experience with autos, and I guess I can manage yours. I ran one like this several times when I was out with Mr. Emberg."

"Den take der vheel," went on Fritsch. "I comes back wid Miss Potter und you can race."

"Oh, Larry! Can you do it?" and Grace looked a little alarmed.

"Of course I can," and the young reporter spoke confidently.

The car was stopped and the change made. Larry soon found he could manage the various levers all right, and that the car responded readily to his guiding hand.

"This must be the place," he said, after they had ridden for half an hour at as high speed as they dared, considering the fact that there were policemen on every other block.

He stopped the car in front of a house that seemed to be uninhabited. It answered the description Retto had given, and Larry knocked on the door. After several minutes the portal opened a crack, showing that it was held by a chain.

"Is Mr. Potter here?" asked Larry, though he knew the missing millionaire was not. The man who had opened the door looked suspiciously at the inquirer. "It's all right," the young reporter went on. "I come from Mr. Retto. I want to aid Mr. Potter."

"You're too late," was the answer. "They've got him into their clutches. They'll work their game before he knows that everything is all right, and that it is safe for him to show himself. If they had only waited half an hour all would have been well. I just got another telephone message from Retto, saying that all matters were satisfactorily adjusted, and that there was no further need for Mr. Potter to hide. But he doesn't know this. I have no way of telling him, and he'll sign the papers before those men will let him go."

"Tell me in which direction they went and I'll go after them!" cried Larry. "They can't have gone far, and we can overtake them in the auto!"

"They have a car, too," replied the man. "A fast one. They managed, by a trick, to get Mr. Potter into it. If I could only get word to him he could laugh at their efforts! If I could only send him a message!"

"What is the message?" asked Larry.

"It is this. 'The money is safe!'"

"Is that all?"

"That's all, but how can you get it to him?"

"Didn't you hear anything that might give you a clue to where the men were going?"

"Somewhere out toward the Orange Mountains. That's all I know. They are going to the home of some lawyer or judge, I believe. There is some legal matter involved."

"Then that's where we'll go!" decided the young reporter, as he hurried back to the auto and told Grace and Fritsch what he had heard.

"On to de mountains!" cried the German reporter. "My car is yours! It will climb de biggest hills on der high gear, und ve will catch de scoundrels!"

Once more they were off. They took the Plank Road to Newark, and, on inquiring in the latter city, learned that a car, answering the description of the one Mr. Potter had been taken off in, had passed about half an hour before.

"That's not so bad!" exclaimed Larry. "We can catch 'em, I guess!"

"I hope so!" murmured Grace.

"If my car doesn't beat de oder one I gives up riding," remarked Fritsch, with proper pride in his machine.

They passed through Newark, and were soon on the road leading to Orange, at the foot of the mountains. The highway was conducive to speed, and Larry "let her out several notches," as he expressed it, at the same time keeping watch for policemen on motorcycles, who were alert to nab the unwary auto speeders.

Every time they saw a car in front of them they were anxious until they saw it was not the one they wanted. They passed a number of machines, and when Orange was reached they had not been successful.

"Now for a mountain climb!" exclaimed Larry, as he slowed down the engine to give the water a chance to cool off before attempting the ascent. "Will it do Eagle Rock hill, Fritsch?"

"I think so," replied the German. "I never tried it, but de circular says it vill do it."

Eagle Rock hill is known far and wide as one of the steepest ascents up which an automobile can be sent. Many cars have to take it on the low gear, or go as slowly as possible. Even then it is a strain.

"Suppose we should overtake them there?" suggested Grace.

"Ve'd catch 'em!" exclaimed the German, with a confidence born of admiration for his car.

On and on they chugged. At the foot of the long, steep slope Larry set the levers on second gear, as he did not want to take any chances with the auto. Up and up they went, their eyesstrained through the dust for the sight of a green car, for that was the color of the machine in which rode the men who had taken Mr. Potter away.

"Hark!" exclaimed Grace, suddenly. "It sounds like an auto just ahead of us!"

"It is," declared Larry, whose quick ear had caught the chug-chug of a motor.

An instant later they had rounded a turn. There, in front of them, climbing the steep hill, was a green car. In it could be seen four men.

"That's them!" cried Larry.

"Open her up! Throw in the high gear!" yelled Fritsch, who was now as enthusiastic and as interested in the chase as were either of his companions. "Let her rip!"

"Will she stand it?" asked Larry, shouting the words over his shoulder to Grace and Fritsch in the tonneau.

"Sure!"

There was a grinding noise as Larry threw in the high-speed gear. The auto hung back for an instant because of the sudden change. The motor seemed to groan at the unexpected load thrown on it. Then, like a gallant horse responding to the call of its rider, the car leaped ahead.

"Hurrah!" cried Larry. "She'll do it! We'll catch 'em!"

The distance between the two cars was lessening. Those in the green machine seemed unaware of the approach of their pursuers.

"Can you see your father?" asked the German of Grace.

"I'm not sure. It looks like him!"

She stood up in the tonneau, holding to the back of the seat in front of her to steady herself against the swaying of the car.

Just then Larry blew a blast on the horn. As the deep tone responded to his pressure on the big rubber bulb the men in the green machine looked back. At the sight of one of the faces Grace cried.

"It's father! It's father!"

Above the noise made by the two autos the millionaire heard his daughter's voice. He stood up and, leaning over the back of the seat, waved his hand to her. Then one of the men sitting beside him forcibly drew the millionaire down.

"Oh! We must get to him!" cried Grace. "They may do him some harm! Hurry, Larry!"

"Shove her over a few more notches!" cried Fritsch. "She'll take more gasolene!"

Larry obeyed the instructions of the German reporter. The car seemed to feel new life and leaped ahead. The distance from the other car was steadily growing less. Fritsch's confidence in his machine was not misplaced. But the men in the green car were making efforts to escape. The chauffeur had advanced his spark, and the car was taking the steep grade almost as well as was that of the pursuers.

"Can't we catch them?" cried Grace, in an agony of doubt and fear.

Larry narrowly watched the green car. He saw that in spite of the efforts of the driver it was losing speed.

"We'll do it," he said, quietly.

Then Larry tried a trick which had come into his mind almost at the last moment. Keeping his car going as fast as possible he steered it so as to pass the other auto. He knew he had speed enough to do it, and realized that he must act quickly, as they were almost at the summit of the hill.

Closer and closer the two cars came together, that driven by the young reporter gaining. Now the front wheels overlapped the rear ones of the green machine—now they were at the side door of the tonneau—now the two tonneaus were even! This was what Larry wanted.

Slowing down his engine the least bit, so as to keep in pace with the other machine and not pass it, he called across to Mr. Potter, as the two autos raced side by side:

"Mr. Potter, I bring you a message from your friends!"

"What is it?"

"It is this! 'The money is safe!'"

"Good!" cried the millionaire. "Now I don't care what these scoundrels do!"

"Father! Father!" cried Grace.

"Stop that machine!" yelled Larry to the chauffeur of the green car.

"You can't make me!" retorted the man.

"Jump into our car!" cried Fritsch to Mr. Potter. "You can do it!"

The two machines were close together, and so evenly were they running that they seemed to be standing still, side by side. The millionaire arose and endeavored to get out of the tonneau, and into that of the auto in which sat his daughter.

"No, you don't!" exclaimed one of the men beside him, and he took hold of Mr. Potter.

"Let me go!" called the rich man. "I'm not afraid of you now. There's no longer any reason for me to remain in hiding!"

"You can't go until you sign those papers!" cried another of the men.

"Stop that car!" shouted Larry again.

"Let's see you make me!" was the impudent retort of the man at the wheel.

"I'll make you!" declared the young reporter.

He gave a quick motion to the steering wheel. Then he shoved the levers over, and pressed down the pedal that cut out the muffler and slightly relieved the strain on the motor. Fritsch's car shot ahead. Larry steered it directly in front of the green machine, and kept just far enough in advance to avoid a collision.

"Get out of the way!" shouted the driver of the emerald car.

"Now I guess you'll stop!" retorted the young reporter.

The road suddenly narrowed. Larry gradually slowed up his car. There was no room to pass, and the other machine had to slacken up also.

Larry suddenly shut off his power and put on the brakes. His machine came to a gradual stop. There was a bump behind and the other had collided with it, but not enough to cause any damage.

"There! I guess you'll stop now!" exclaimed Larry, as he leaped from his seat and hurried back to the green car.

But the men did not await his coming. With a shout to his companions the chauffeur of the rear auto leaped out. The others followed his example, leaving Mr. Potter alone in the automobile.

"Father! Father!" cried Grace.

"Is this really you, Mr. Potter?" asked the reporter, hardly able to believe that he had found the missing millionaire.

"That's who I am!" exclaimed the man whom Larry had sought so long. Mr. Potter entered the other machine and clasped Grace into his arms. "I'm back from my enforced exile," he went on. "Now you can send the story to your paper."

"I must get to a telephone!" cried Larry, his newspaper instincts to the fore again, now that he had successfully covered his special assignment.

"Get back into my car," suggested Fritsch. "Dere is a telephone at de top of der hill. I'll drive you now so long as de race is ofer!"

"And we won!" cried Grace. "Oh, father! How glad I am to have you back!"

"How glad I am to get back!" replied Mr. Potter.

Larry sat beside the German reporter, who took his place at the steering wheel. The other car was left where the men had abandoned it. They had disappeared into the woods on either side of the road, and never troubled Mr. Potter again.

"Why did you disappear, Mr. Potter?" asked Larry, who had to have some facts to telephone in, as it was near first edition-time.

"It's a long story to tell, young man," replied the millionaire, "and quite complicated. Briefly, I had to disappear in order to save a number of widows and orphans from losing what little money they depended on for a living. As you have probably guessed, I am interested in many financial matters. One was the building of an extension of the subway. Hundreds of widows, and guardians of orphans, had bought stock in this enterprise, as it was sold by popular subscription.

"While abroad I learned there was a scheme on foot to involve me in certain legal difficulties, and it might even cause my arrest in order to get me to do certain things that would force the price of the subway stock down, and so bankrupt many innocent persons. To prevent this I determined to disappear, without even the knowledge of my family. How I managed it I will tell you later. Matters were going along all right until Retto, whose real name, you might as well know, is Simonson, suddenly disappeared. I did not know what to do, nor how matters, with which I had entrusted him, were progressing. But it wasn't his fault. I wonder what happened to him?"

Larry explained about Mr. Simonson's accident, of which Mr. Potter was ignorant.

"When these men, my enemies, unexpectedly appeared to-day at the house where I had been hiding ever since I disappeared, asked me to appear in a New Jersey court, I had to go with them," went on Mr. Potter. "It was in the nature of an arrest, and I did not dare disobey. They wanted to take me before a Supreme Court Justice in his home on the mountain and make me sign certain papers.

"But you came along in the nick of time. When you gave me that message to the effect that the money was all right, I knew that the affairs of the subway had been so arranged that the stock would not go down and the widows and orphans would not suffer. I was willing then to appear in court, as the schemes of the scoundrels, who had practically kidnapped me, could amount to nothing. But it seems they didn't wait to see what the outcome would be. I'm much obliged to you, Larry."

"So am I," added Grace, with a smile.

"I'd do it all over again for the sake of getting such a good story—and—er—of course, finding you and helping your daughter," Larry finished. "Now to telephone this in."

Mr. Emberg could hardly believe the news that Larry fairly shouted over the wire.

"Found him, you say! Good for you, Larry. It'll be a great beat! Wait a minute! I'll let Harvey take the story. Talk fast. Give us enough for the first edition, and then, for the second, get the whole story from Mr. Potter. This is a corker!"

What a scene there was in the *Leader* office then! Mr. Newton grabbed up paper and pencil and rushed to the telephone booth to which Larry's wire had been switched so that the story could be taken with fewer interruptions. Page after page of notes did Mr. Newton scribble down, as Larry dictated the dramatic finding of the missing millionaire during the automobile chase.

"That'll do, Larry!" cried Mr. Newton, when he had the first half of the story. "I'll get one of the other boys to take the rest while I grind this out on the machine."

So the young reporter dictated the remainder of the account to another person in the *Leader* office, while Mr. Newton was pounding away on the typewriter at his section.

Thus it went on in relays. The first part of the story was in type before Larry had finished his end of it. Then, as there was no more time to get anything further in for the first edition, Larry went back to where he had left Mr. Potter, Grace and Fritsch in the automobile. Mr. Potter gave the young reporter some additional particulars.

He explained that he had learned, while in Europe, of a mix-up in New York politics that involved his company, which was building the new subway line. Sullivan, Kilburn and Reilly were factors in the game, and the control of the assembly district would go to whoever could bring about the opening of the new subway route through it.

Mr. Potter repeated, more at detail, how there was likely to be a big law-suit over the matter, which would tie up operations for a year, and which would force down the price of the stock so that many small investors would lose all they owned.

"I had promised Sullivan to do as he wanted, in case he supported Reilly," Mr. Potter went on. "Later I found I could not do as I had agreed without getting tangled up in the legal conflict. They wanted to serve certain papers on me, and get me into the jurisdiction of the law courts, so I decided, in order to protect those who were unable to protect themselves, to disappear. I was aware that a wrong construction might be placed on it, that it would subject me to much criticism, that it would be hard and that it would cause distress to my family and friends. But there was no other way in which I could aid the helpless, so I decided to do it."

The millionaire explained how he had sailed from Italy under an assumed name, after arranging there with his friend, Mr. Simonson, to precede him to New York, do certain work, and keep him informed of how matters went. Simonson took the name Mah Retto, which had a foreign sound, and could be depended upon to deceive Mr. Potter's enemies. Mr. Simonson was of dark complexion and looked like an East Indian. The name was formed from some of the letters making up the millionaire's name. Retto's handwriting was very similar to that of Mr. Potter's, and easily passed for it, even under the scrutiny of Grace and her mother. The man himself bore a remarkable resemblance to the millionaire and nearly deceived Grace once.

Most unexpectedly, some of Mr. Potter's enemies got on the trail of Retto, and he learned they would be waiting for him when he landed in New York. He decided to elude them.

He was aboard the *Olivia* when the ship struck on the bar, and resolved to take a desperate chance and come ashore on a life-raft. He did, and Larry and Bailey rescued him. Then followed his shaving off of his moustache in the fisherman's hut to make a good disguise, and Larry's subsequent chase after him. Once Larry had been close on Mr. Potter's trail. The millionaire was in Retto's room the night Larry called on the mysterious man in the Jackson tenement, and this explained the reference in the letter to the young reporter being so "close" after Mr. Potter.

Sullivan, it was explained, had an idea that Grace or her mother knew where Mr. Potter was hiding, and was much disappointed because the rich man could not carry out the original plan of political action.

"I think Sullivan will show himself, now that he knows I have been found," said Grace's father. "He has been looking for me on his own responsibility, I understand. I have straightened matters out so that he can support Reilly as he promised to do, Larry, in that interview he gave you. I think that was all he wanted me to come back for.

"Sullivan used to go up and watch my house," Mr. Potter went on. "He thought I was there, I suppose. Retto also watched it, but for a different purpose. I sent him up to catch glimpses of my wife and daughter, to see if they were all right, as I did not dare venture into that neighborhood for fear of being recognized. I had their miniatures, however. The night I reached New York I went to the house and got them. I remained in the suburbs of Jersey City most of the time, as, until to-day, the scoundrels did not have matters so arranged that they could legally serve papers on me in New Jersey. They must have taken a last desperate chance this morning, but, thanks to you, Larry, they were foiled."

In Fritsch's auto, after Larry had finished telephoning in the story, the little party returned to New York. They took Mr. Simonson, or Retto, from the hospital to Mr. Potter's house. There he explained his part in aiding the millionaire. Larry gave him back the papers he had secured from Captain Tantrella, and the curious gold coin Mr. Simonson had lost from his watch chain in the fisherman's hut.

Mr. Simonson told his employer how he had tried to run away from Larry that day on the pier, as matters were then not yet ripe for a disclosure, and how he had fallen under the horses' feet.

"When you came to see me in the hospital," he went on to Larry, "I was about to send for Mr. Potter, for I felt I was in bad shape and that the mystery might now come to an end. Then I became unconscious, was delirious for three weeks, and the next I knew was when the nurse told me this morning that the day after to-morrow you were coming to see me. I decided I must communicate with Mr. Potter. But when I called him up, I was startled when I was told by the man in whose house he was hiding that his enemies had him."

"But Larry got me away from them," went on Mr. Potter, with a happy laugh. "This ends the mystery of my disappearance."

"I must telegraph mother the good news," said Grace. "She is in Lakewood. I had also better notify the private detective that he need no longer work on the case."

"We'll go to Lakewood and surprise your mother," said her father. "I need a rest after my hard work in keeping away from Larry Dexter. I'll telephone the detective agency. I suppose the manager will be disappointed that a newspaper man beat him," which was exactly how the manager felt.

The young reporter, bidding Grace and her father good-bye, returned to the office of the *Leader*, going down in Fritsch's auto.

"Well, you have given us some news!" exclaimed Mr. Emberg. "Look at that!"

He held up the paper, the front page of which was almost all taken up with the story of the missing millionaire.

"I suppose that ends my special assignment, then."

"This one is finished," spoke the city editor, "but I may have another for you."

"What kind?"

"I'll tell you later."

Those of my readers who want to know what Larry's next assignment was may learn by reading the fourth volume of this series, to be called: "Larry Dexter and the Bank Mystery, or, A Young Reporter in Wall Street." In that story we shall follow the young reporter through adventures which were exciting in the extreme.

The *Leader* beat every other paper in New York on the Potter story, and Larry was the hero of the occasion. The next day he located Sullivan and cleared up that end of the case.

"I suppose you'd like to take a short rest?" said Mr. Emberg to the young reporter a few days later. "You had quite a strenuous time of it in that automobile race."

"I guess I could stand a little vacation."

"Then you shall have it."

Larry wondered where he would spend the vacation, but the matter was settled for him. When he got home that night he found a telegram awaiting him. It was from Grace Potter, and read:

"Can't you come down to Lakewood for a few days? Mother and father would be glad to see you. So would I."

Larry went.

End of the book.

www.ingramcontent.com/pod-product-compliance
Lightning Source LLC
Chambersburg PA
CBHW070652290526
45790CB00001B/286